7 SUMMITS

**1 CORNISHMAN CLIMBING THE HIGHEST
MOUNTAINS ON EACH CONTINENT**

ED BUCKINGHAM

With thanks
ejbuckingham

7 SUMMITS

1 CORNISHMAN CLIMBING THE HIGHEST MOUNTAINS ON EACH CONTINENT

ED BUCKINGHAM

CRESCENT
HOUSE

Sheffield
www.v-publishing.co.uk

7 SUMMITS
ED BUCKINGHAM

First published in 2016 by Crescent House.

CRESCENT HOUSE
Crescent House, 228 Psalter Lane, Sheffield, S11 8UT.
www.v-publishing.co.uk

This book is a work of non-fiction based on the life of Ed Buckingham.
The author has stated to the publishers that, except in such minor
respects not affecting the substantial accuracy of the work, the contents
of the book are true.

A CIP catalogue record for this book is available from the British Library.

ISBN: 978-1-909461-49-9 (Paperback)
ISBN: 978-1-909461-50-5 (Ebook)

Design and production by Jane Beagley. Cover design by Nathan Ryder.
Vertebrate Publishing.
www.v-publishing.co.uk

Crescent House is committed to printing on paper from sustainable sources.

Printed and bound in the UK by T.J. International Ltd, Padstow, Cornwall.

This book is dedicated to those people who suffer
from an undeserved illness. Children that are born or
contract an illness at an early age. Consequently this has
a detrimental effect on the way they live the rest of their lives.
Also to those that have lived their lives without abusing their
bodies and who work hard for the good of their families.

CONTENTS

CHAPTER 1

THE ROOF OF AFRICA

Never have I experienced this environment, culture and altitude.

— ED BUCKINGHAM

My trek to Kilimanjaro, Tanzania, in 1999, was like no holiday I had experienced before – the poor hygiene, the food, the lack of privacy and experiencing the culture of a developing country were all challenges I had to face. Kilimanjaro is best known for being climbable for those with little more than walking experience. It is the easiest of the seven continental summits and an increasing number of climbers and walkers travel to Africa with this in mind.

Kilimanjaro is very much like an island surrounded by the hot and dry plains of the Masai. From Kilimanjaro's base, the mountain rises 5,985 metres to its icy summit – quite a challenge for somebody coming from a county where the highest tor is Brown Willy, which stands at 420 metres, a mere pittance in comparison. Kilimanjaro sits inside Tanzania, bordering Kenya 400 kilometres south of the equator. It is widely believed that Queen Victoria gave the mountain to her German grandson, Kaiser Wilhelm II, which explains the curve in what is otherwise a ruler-straight border between the two countries. As Tanzania, formerly known as Tanganyika, then became a part of German East Africa, German colonials were the first to explore Kilimanjaro. When World War One ended in 1918, the mountain became a British asset once again until Tanganyika became independent in 1961. In 1964, Tanganyika became part of the United Republic of Tanganyika and Zanzibar, and changing its name to the United Republic of Tanzania within a year.

The vast slopes of Kilimanjaro are fairly unusual as they pass through many different climatic worlds. On Kibo, the highest volcanic cone, climbers travel through tropical rainforest, heathland, desert and finally tundra before reaching the ice-bound summit, all in the space of a few days. The best times to climb Kilimanjaro are between December and early March, and from June to October. This is so that climbers miss two rainy seasons. It is imperative that climbers are prepared for cold weather and sudden storms because higher up it becomes very cold, especially from June to August, which is the East African winter. It often becomes very windy and the temperatures reach as low as minus ten degrees.

The summit of Kibo rises steeply for 180 metres from the floor of the caldera. Uhuru is the apex of the great southern glaciers that spill down the south side of Kibo, providing some of the most challenging climbs. Between the Western Breach (Arrow Glacier) Route and the Heim Glacier is the Breach Wall, a 600-metre precipice of crumbling overhanging rock, which is considered to be the hardest route on Kilimanjaro.

On the opposite side of the mountain is the Northern Icefield, a single expanse of ice that drapes over the crater rim. Its shimmering whiteness is visible high above the Amboseli National Park in neighbouring Kenya. Other glaciers lurk languidly in the shallow crater, like beached whales hopelessly waiting for the next ice age to secure their survival. All of the glaciers on Kilimanjaro are in retreat and some have disappeared altogether. Like much of Africa the records of human activity on Kilimanjaro begin with the arrival of missionaries whose travels took them on to the mountain in the nineteenth century. Of course, it may well have been climbed by these early residents of the region. Undoubtedly, the great volcano with its strange white cap would have been entangled with the native superstitions and folklore. In 1887 missionary, Charles New, became the first to reach snow on Kilimanjaro when he climbed to the saddle between Kibo and Mawenzi. The first actual ascent to Uhuru Peak (then named Kaiser Wilhelm Spitze) was made in 1889, by German Geologist Hans Meyer, Austrian mountaineer Ludwig Purtscheller, and a local man called Lauwo.

There are six moorland approaches to the base of Kibo. They are Marangu, Mweka, Umbwe, Machame, Shira and Rongai, but only Marangu, otherwise known as the Tourist Route, takes a climber all the way to Uhuru Peak, ascending slowly for 1,182 metres. All of the other routes lead to the Kibo Circuit Path, which joins the rest of the routes to the summit. As well as Marangu, there are other climbs that do not require technical mountaineering skills such as the Barafu and the Western Breach route, however, the latter can be extremely difficult when covered in snow.

We climbed in September to avoid the rainy seasons, taking the Machame route up and descending down Mweka on a nine-day trek. This was the longest route but it allowed our bodies more time to acclimatise. We took the 'walk high, sleep low' approach. Given where I came from, high altitude was outside my experience. Walking at high altitude affects people in many different ways, regardless of a person's fitness and mountaineering knowledge. Decreased oxygen concentration in the blood, caused by the lower atmospheric pressure found at higher elevations, creates oedema, the swelling and pooling of body fluid. When this occurs in the brain or lungs, the results can be devastating. The best cure for any onslaught of altitude sickness is to descend quickly, to a point where the air is thicker with oxygen.

Kibo, Mawenzi and Shira are Kilimanjaro's three peaks. Kibo is the highest with its recognisable volcanic cone. Its summit crater is some 2,500 metres across. It's this feature where the majority of climbs are done.

East of Kibo stands the jagged spire of Mawenzi, the second highest peak, which also offers numerous rock-climbs. The third peak is Shira, lying to the west of Kibo. It is so eroded that it is little more than a plateau of rolling heathland. Kibo's crater rim is intact except for the mighty slit of the Western Breach and much smaller notches on the eastern side. These notches provide the easiest access to the crater and rim.

Ludwig Purtscheller and Johannes Korner opened the ever-popular tourist (Marangu) route in 1898. The Kibo Hut, built in 1932, offered shelter to many an adventurer and its location, at 4,700 metres, made it instrumental in the increase in tourism. There are a multitude of huts in the area today and also lower down the trail at Mandara and Horombo. The first ascent of the Western Breach was made in 1953 by a University of Sheffield team. In 1957, A. Nelson, H. Cooke and D. Goodall made the first ascent of the classic Heim Glacier Route. Most of the other major lines were climbed during the 1970s, mainly by the visiting teams from the mountain clubs of Kenya. In 1978, Reinhold Messner along with Konrad Renzler climbed the formidable Breach Wall direct route.

More than 50,000 people visit Kilimanjaro per year, making conservation a real issue. The mountain is showing signs of erosion on trails. Litter and human waste is especially apparent near the lesser-known camps and there are signs of deforestation caused by the cutting of trees to make firewood. Sanitation is not yet a problem but the toilets at Kibo Hut have upset even the strongest of stomachs. At the moment, very little is being done to eliminate the environmental problems on trails. The National Park Authority, with the support of local and overseas agencies, could ban the use of firewood and encourage the use of gas and kerosene stoves. Visitors should also be asked to collect their litter.

Arriving at the Ndarakwai camp, at midnight, I met up with the rest of the team and we ate supper outside, on long tables, before our first night on trek.

How many times in Cornwall do you sit outside at midnight to eat a meal? The group comprised about forty-three clients, many of whom were from England – couples and individuals of a variety of ages. With the guides and support staff, there were around 110 of us altogether. I went to sleep on a camp bed, which I thought was pure luxury and under white, stiff, starched sheets, I slept like a baby. The international travel from England, the transfers and the time zone difference meant everybody was feeling the effects of tiredness. Early introductions were civil but a good night's rest was high on the agenda.

The next day began early at 6 a.m. which would become our normal waking hour on trek. The porters came round with an early morning milky cup of tea. The porters were local tribespeople, looking to earn a living far and above what they were accustomed to. The sight of their cheery, smiling happy faces never failed to delight me. They never came inside the privacy of my tent, they just peered in, waiting for me to hand out my personalised mug. They would do anything asked of them such as simple tasks like washing and carrying luggage.

After breakfast, we made our way in a convoy of Land Cruisers to register at Landorossi. We had to register as a group before going into the National Park. This was the end of vehicular travel. From this point on, we travelled on foot. At the start of the walk, we travelled through rainforest and saw a wide variety of exotic plants and animals. One of the most spectacular plants was the giant groundsel, which has tree-like stems holding large rosettes of leaves as high as five metres. Stopping for lunch in the rainforest, I was astonished to see a picnic had been laid out with enough food for all of us. Before the trip I had been worried about missing my regular intake of fruit and what I would do if there were nuts. I had read nuts were popular because of their nutritional value and edibility after being carried and squashed. I had even brought flapjack as a substitute but, like my powder drink, it had become congealed and sticky.

Feeling content, we carried on walking until we reached the spot where we would spend our first night under canvas, in a clearing in the rainforest (at just under 3,000 metres). The porters had already set up our tents and placed our belongings inside. Dinner consisted of stew and spaghetti. I was amazed how a meal like that could be produced for so many people in this environment. The porters broke down and packed up camp. On trek, they overtook the rest of us, carrying loads weighing eighty kilograms. Standing to the side, I watched them running past, bent double. Many of them were not wearing shoes but they were always smiling. With an existence like this, their life expectancy dropped dramatically.

That night, a ranger patrolled the camp as we slept, to protect us from wild animals. I shared a tent with Paul Stevenson, an IT specialist from Wales. We were roughly the same age but he had more climbing experience than me, having spent a fair amount of time in North Wales. We were both the same sort of build; neither of us had suffered the hardship of going long without a meal.

Breakfast the next day consisted of porridge, omelette and toast. We carried on through the rainforest, listening to the sounds of the birds in the trees and smelling the freshness of the forest. It was a relatively short day of walking and once we left the rainforest, we came out into a tropical area, which was open and vast. Standing before me looking massively impressive was Kilimanjaro. It was so huge with just a wisp of cloud going across the crater, like a man enjoying his pipe. This was the backdrop to the next camp, at just over 3,000 metres. There was a long way to walk and climb before I got anywhere near the summit but I was enjoying it. Things were going well up until this point but there was still a long way to go. We had now left the security and coverage of the rainforest and were walking across open moorland and heathland. So far this had not been a problem but we were walking a lot slower than normal.

That afternoon we had the choice of resting or going on an acclimatisation walk to the Shira Plateau. Some people were now suffering altitude sickness. We could take a drug called Diamox to help us acclimatise quicker but I chose not to because it causes significant side effects such as diarrhoea, vomiting and tingling in the fingers and toes. I chose instead to drink four to six litres of water per day and combat headaches by taking ibuprofen. We learnt from the leaders shouting 'pole, pole', which means 'slowly, slowly', that it was frowned upon to walk ahead of them. This is a common habit of bullish English walkers – rambling ahead, oblivious of the altitude and group discipline.

On day four, we saw the first frost on the tents and the team broke out their thermals. Walking speeds varied in such a large group. Paul and I found ourselves walking in a quicker group of around ten people, two of which were Ben and Vince with whom I would do a few trips. That morning was the hardest climb yet as we ascended to our next camp at around 3,500 metres. After dinner, I travelled with a group to Jonsell Point and began chatting with Juliet Davies, who was, at one time, the swimming champion of Wales. Juliet told me she was feeling her fitness levels depleting because walking was not enough exercise for her. I did not feel the same way but we decided to jog together to Jonsell Point. So far, I was feeling great and held no qualms about our pace, preferring to save energy for the days ahead. Under the clearing skies, I went to bed earlier. Once the sun set, the temperature plummeted and I craved the warmth of my sleeping bag. I savoured the sunsets like hot summers in Cornwall.

We were greeted by the clearest views of Kilimanjaro on day five. It was a beautiful morning. I had left a cotton T-shirt and gaiters out overnight and they were now stiff as a board – how I laughed at my stupidity. Over the course of time, I invested in clothing high in wicking material. When our bodies perspire, cotton has the effect of holding on to the moisture and cools the body quicker, whereas clothing that wicks pulls moisture away from the body and keeps the body warm. Cotton is also difficult to dry, particularly in harsh, cold conditions. My concerns before joining up were having adequate washing facilities over the course of the holiday. Growing up I had suffered from eczema especially in between my toes and on the backs of my legs. Exasperated by the conditions and environment I thought it would have a detrimental effect on my body. I had invested around 2,000 pounds in this trip and I had paid for new gear like rucksacks, sleeping bags and trekking boots. At the time, I thought it was a fair commitment for something I may not enjoy doing. The money was not a problem as I had regular full-time employment and still lived at home with my parents.

Porridge was now a firm favourite of mine, because it filled me up and released energy slowly which is ideal for walking and long days in the hills. We now walked towards Shira Cathedral, scaling a ridge at 3700 metres. At twenty-five degrees Celsius, this was the hottest day of our trek so far, so I made sure I drank more and covered my head. Pre-trip, the heat and the altitude had been my biggest fears. At home, I find it hard going when it is hot and I conscientiously cover up my head and neck.

We now noticed a lack of flora and fauna. We had entered an area covered with volcanic rocks that were formed many years ago. They were very hot under the heat of the sun and sitting on them felt like sitting on heated seats in a modern car. When we camped later that day (at just under 4,000 metres), we were sheltered beneath the backdrop of Kibo and in the forefront of Jonsell Point and Shira Cathedral.

As we stood at the foot of Kilimanjaro the next morning, there was no frost because we were sheltered under Kibo. Today's climb would take us to 4,330 metres. Today we were more exposed to the wind and it was noticeably colder. We were walking for longer periods each day, using more energy and burning more calories. The previous days of drinking lots of fluid and maintaining a disciplined approach to walking were paying dividends now. More energy is required when climbing at high altitude and it takes its toll on the body. After lunch we passed down the Barranco Valley. We often walked high and dropped down into a camp because this is best way to acclimatise and we did benefit from it.

Even though Kilimanjaro is huge and has many routes we now found ourselves sharing camp with other companies. It made us extra careful because not everyone was hygiene aware. The camp became a little dirtier and was covered with rubbish and human waste. You would think that people would leave the mountain as they found it. I have always been brought up to take litter home with me.

Because we had dropped the previous day, we had quite a climb up the Barranco Wall, before starting along a ridge. The weather was cloudy and the breeze felt raw. When we stopped for a period of time, I put on another layer of clothing to harness the heat generated from the exertion of the climb. Towards the end of the ridge, we dropped down steeply into the next valley, called Karranga, where we had lunch. I learnt not to stuff myself with food at lunchtime because walking on a full stomach does not make the climb up any easier. Soon we were climbing up a scree slope with the sun beating down.

Day eight was the final push before making a summit attempt. Our group seemed very strong; nobody appeared to be struggling, but I don't think any of us would have admitted it if we were. We walked on, chatting about home and our lives. My companions envied where I came from; Cornwall is such a beautiful place. A few of them said they had second homes there. It was the first time I had ever truly appreciated my home county. I was comforted and encouraged by the camaraderie. It was by far the toughest day, especially in the afternoon when we travelled to Barafu Ridge at 5,000 metres. Whereas before we had dropped down after walking to a greater height, this would not be the case from now. Consequently, for the first time, people were showing signs of tiredness and altitude sickness. We camped for the final time and in preparation for making our summit attempt, we only got a few hours' rest.

Throughout the trip, I felt strong because I had listened to the leaders, drunk lots of water and enjoyed the food. However, I was still approaching the summit with caution. To get this far was good but we would be ascending in the dark after camping for several days with limited washing facilities and amenities. Even on Kilimanjaro, the oxygen levels are reduced. It felt good being among like-minded people who all had the same goal. We were told to pack light and share items like cameras and first aid kits. Paul and I packed a few bits into a rucksack for the summit, including a camera and some water. Because our group was so large, we staggered our summit attempts to avoid congestion among ourselves and other groups. I was too excited to get much sleep. I was filled with adrenaline. It did not occur to me that I would not summit. I had not exerted myself beyond my limit and I was feeling confident. However, the thought of suffering altitude sickness and having to turn back was in the back of my mind.

I chatted to different people each day. Colin and Peggy were from East Preston in West Sussex. They owned a shop retailing walking and mountaineering equipment. Now their children had grown up, they were taking the opportunity to travel and do things they had always wanted to. Summiting Kilimanjaro was a dream they both shared. Emma lived in Braunton, Devon, not far from me. She was young and petite and her boyfriend had just proposed to her but he had not come away on this trip. Until now, it had not been apparent that walking was a problem for her and every now and then she became very emotional. As I didn't know her very well, I was not sure whether she was genuinely upset or whether the altitude was affecting her. Luciano was an Italian living in North London.

He had good looks, designer clothes and was a bit of ladies' man. He soon struck up a noticeable affection for Juliet. Harry was from Belfast in Ireland, he was loud and forthright in all of his opinions. After summiting Kilimanjaro, boy did he party on the spice island of Zanzibar. Making his entrance at the resort he ran past reception and jumped into the pool fully clothed. Mind you, I do not think that I was far behind him.

Leaving at around 1 a.m. we made our way, by the light of our head torches, up a frozen scree slope. I could see the lights ahead of me traversing upwards, winding like a snake under the stars. It was cold but I felt toasty tucked up in my balaclava, fleece and gloves. I was fuelled with energy and anticipation. I had walked most of the journey at the front behind the leader, but now I found myself at the back of the group. Liz and Mike Davies, from the Lake District, had been walking strongly until this point but now Liz was really struggling with the side effects of using Diamox. Clearly embarrassed by her incapacity, I stayed with her to offer words of encouragement and assurance. I like helping others and it was giving me satisfaction now. I could feel her confidence growing as we walked on at a pace she was comfortable with.

With the red skyline of dawn, we reached the rim at Stella Point. It was not yet 5.30 a.m. and to have got this far up the steep scree slope was good. Many people reach Stella Point thinking they have got to the summit but there is still a little way to go. I was too excited to feel tired and cold. Liz felt weak from dehydration and altitude sickness but with me by her side, she was still walking up towards the summit. As we walked through the fields of ice, which stood upright like stalks of maize in a field, it felt so surreal and made me feel small and insignificant. These fields of ice stood so high that we could not peer over them and look around. For some strange reason I expected to see polar bears. I could have spent all day up there. To me it looked like a magical kingdom in Neverland. Walking to

Uhuru Point was easy, because the ground was flat with a gentle slope up to the sign. Liz and I beamed as we made it to the top with the others at 5,895 metres – the highest point in Africa. I was ecstatic, my feeling of achievement was overwhelming but I managed to refrain from crying in front of everybody. Paul had our shared camera and took photographs.

After taking our shots and doing a 360-degree walk of the summit to admire the views, it was time to descend. I was disappointed because I wanted to revel in my achievement a little bit longer. After spending so long trekking up, why were we turning round and going down so quickly? As we descended, many more people were making their way to the summit including members from our party. Their faces were probably a mirror image of ours an hour ago – tired, dirty, red and puffy from the exertion of the climb. Our jubilance and words of encouragement energised them and, with newfound vigour, they staggered on towards their own glories.

We travelled the same way down and it now became obvious why we had travelled up in the dark: the frozen scree slope had thawed and some of the rocks had become loose and trying to climb it in the light would have been demoralising, arduous and energy-sapping. After a short stop at camp, it was time to go down further. It is best to descend as far as possible so as not to be affected by the altitude. We went down to Mweka camp, at 3,500 metres, where I ate and celebrated with a very small amount of alcohol, which went straight to my head. The porters found it very funny – I was a very cheap date indeed! I went to bed shattered, exhausted and drunk.

The next day, we walked the remaining way out of the park, before we were picked up and taken back to Ndarakwai lodge. It felt weird being back where we started just over a week ago. Dirty, weary but happy we enjoyed the last night at the lodge before going back to suburbia. Regaling each other with our stories, we laughed under the skies of the African setting sun.

I could not wait to share my adventure with my family and friends back home. This experience would remain with me forever – the challenges, the walking, the camping, the environmental difficulties, the euphoria of summiting and the camaraderie between all of us journeying with one objective in mind.

We spent the next week visiting local communities, going on safari and visiting Zanzibar for some sun and relaxation. I found going into the communities really intimidating. There we were as Westerners, intruding with our Rolex watches and flashy cameras, snapping away like the paparazzi. The local people were clearly poor and earning a living was hard for them. This is why many become porters on Kilimanjaro. A minority then become guides which is a highly thought of and much sought after career in Africa. Coming from Cornwall, I had never seen poverty on this scale before. My camera stayed in my pocket and I stayed outside, choosing not to go into their homes. Truth be known, all I wanted was to go home, back to my family and Cornwall. I had had a fantastic and wonderful experience, far and above anything else I had experienced at the tender age of twenty-six, and I was keen for more.

CHAPTER 2

GROWING UP

*Edward was content as a child as long as
you fed him regularly and changed his nappy.*

— JEAN BUCKINGHAM

I was born Edward James Buckingham, in December 1972, to my proud
parents, Desmond and Jean Buckingham. I was not a small baby by any
means and getting food down me was not a problem. Having been fed,
I would be content and could be put to bed without any trouble. I was
born and raised in Saltash, where I still live today. My mother would push
me up and down the street in my Sherman-type pram. I was quite happy,
dressed in blue, grinning while she struggled up the Cornish hills laden
with shopping. People used to look at me admiringly and say, 'What a
gorgeous baby. Is it a boy or a girl?'

There is a saying in life, 'those you love the most go first.' This was true
for me, I adored two of my grandparents, but they passed away while I
was still young. I spent a lot of time with my Grandad Hambly on holidays and, when I was in my teens, we would watch the local football team,
Saltash United, at Kimberley Stadium. I used to holiday with him in
Lanreath. He made me porridge in the mornings with just a hint of sugar
so that I would eat it without giving him aggro.

When I walk around Cornwall now, I think of him pulling me in my yellow tow truck. He never complained, pulling me miles and walking the dog too. I spent hours out with him in the garden or diving into his shed, oblivious to the rats scurrying about and never bothering to wear gloves or protective clothing. There would be uproar these days. I used to vigorously polish the covers on the wheels of his Ford Escort so I could see my face in them. I would watch him working methodically, offering to help, especially with the manual lifting.

He also took me to Looe for days out on the beach. I used to follow him around the maze of streets to a particular bakery where he bought fresh, homemade pasties. Talland was a favourite village of his, between Hannafore and Polperro. It is a quaint little place with a small beach and a seasonal cafe. It was a place of solitude and quietness and a place of reflection and perspective. I have often thought of him when training for these mountains. He would have been beside himself with worry over some of my challenges. I am not sure I could have put him through it, such was the affection and high esteem I held for him. He was a man forever at ease in his beloved Cornwall. To this day, Looe and Lanreath are sentimental to me. When he passed away, he was missed greatly by his family, especially his sister, who he used to pop in on most days.

We did have a scare when I was two. On Boxing Day he was shelling Brazil nuts and feeding them to me. The gannet I was, as fast as he shelled them, I put them in my mouth, until I started choking and there was an almighty panic to get to a doctor on Boxing Day. It was then my parents found out I had a nut allergy. I would go around saying, 'Not those dam 'zil nuts Grandad.' I truly idolised him and more so after he died and I learnt of his ailments, including a bullet wound to the hand, which he sustained during the Second World War. During all the time I knew him, I never heard him complain. He went on to work for Cornwall County Council, operating pneumatic tools. Until his retirement, his co-workers never knew he was actually registered disabled because he never moaned or shirked away from any responsibilities. Staying at his house in Lanreath, I used to lift open the children's gate at the bottom of the stairs to let him go up. I do not think he truly grasped what strength I had and that I would study him and copy his movements.

In my earlier years, I did struggle with the concept that 'A hat is a hat and not an animal'. My Granny Hambly wore a brown fur hat with a long tail. I used to jump up and down upon it vigorously, in an effort to kill it before proceeding to cook it in a saucepan. Would animal rights approve today? Would Bear Grylls have appreciated my resourcefulness?

Granny Buckingham had an engaging smile that radiated warmth. She cooked the most sought-after quiche and sausage rolls in the Aga, and certainly knew how to win my affections: she just needed to keep supplying me with food. I used to enjoy visiting at Christmas time, playing hide and seek in the garden with my brother. After lunch, we would go out into the nearby woods for a walk in wellingtons, kicking our way through the fallen leaves and pine cones. Returning, we would play with the hand bells around the open fire. My sense of timing has never been very good. I was completely hopeless.

I remember visiting her one Sunday afternoon in Scott Hospital in Plymouth. Getting down from my chair, I knocked the seat, revealing a built-in bowl or commode. The look on my face was pure amazement and surprise. I was never the sharpest tool in the tool box. My gran cried with laughter. Little did I know, those types of toilets would be a significant feature of my holidays in years to come.

My father was born on a farm at Widegates, Looe. He has always enjoyed rural life and the countryside. Even though he never took the farm on, it remains an integral part of his life. Rural life always played a significant part in our family. He served an apprenticeship in the dockyards of

Plymouth as an engineer and machinist. Later, he worked for Astra and Plymouth Skill Centre at Plympton. I used to wake up with him in the morning to see him off to work. Mornings were never a problem for me as I would spend time reading until it was time for school.

I spent hours with my father at weekends on his allotment or on farms where he used to repair and make machinery. I have never been afraid to ask my father for advice and still do to this day. I can always be certain that his opinion will be different to everybody else's, whether his advice is serious or quirky. On one occasion I remember, when I was around fifteen, he gave me the talk about the birds and the bees while I was leaning over a gate, watching a bull go round some heifers.

When doing the weekly shopping at Tesco, I asked why there was such a choice of dog food. His reply was, 'Hmm yes son. You just know it's all going to end up on the streets.' I often wondered where he got his sense of humour from. It was not until his mother died that it struck me. Waiting for the funeral cortege to arrive, I was in the kitchen with Grandad. He looked up at me and said, 'She gave me a good life. There was no television back then, we just used to go to bed early.' To say I was a bit taken back is an understatement.

My little brother Christopher came along. Going to see him for the first time I said, 'Can't we leave him and take a girl instead?' I was adamant that I wanted a little sister. Perhaps it had something to do with being fed up with my being likened to a girl as a baby. We used to squabble as youngsters but we respect and get on with each other now. He says that over the course of time I grew up a lot. I say I was just preparing him for later life with my words of wisdom.

I went to the local Primary School, St Stephens in Saltash. I integrated well with the other children but Mrs Ruse could not always get me to do what she wanted. Every day we drank a pint of milk mid-morning through a straw. It had a thick layer of skin on top that I hated. I got into the habit of sticking my fingers down my throat to make myself sick so she would send me outside, where I really wanted to be. Recently, after many years, I caught up with Mrs Ruse. She was thrilled that one of her pupils has gone on to achieve so much. She said she could not remember me excelling in anything, but I always had a go.

I participated in sports but I was never very capable. 'It's the taking part that counts,' became my favourite line whenever I came last or was the last to be picked in team sports. However, I was a competent swimmer, having been taught from the age of six by an instructor in Central Park, Plymouth. Being able to swim is such a valuable skill. It opens the door to so many activities and team-building events. When people say that they cannot swim or that they are afraid of the water, I think of how much they are missing out on, especially because Cornwall is surrounded by coastline. I used to have this rather worrying habit of going underwater if I knew people were watching me and not resurfacing for several minutes. I half expected one of the supervisors to dive in to rescue me but they never did. Maybe they couldn't swim and that's why they had those long poles, to hook people out.

The headmaster, Mr Hassell, was good musically and directed plays. I joined in and on one occasion kept the play going without the aid of prompts. Playing the role of a grumpy old lock keeper, the main lead forgot his lines so I improvised and the audience never picked up on the momentary pause. One parent came a second night, not to see his son but to see me. My mother did say that at the age of six I decided I did not need to go to school anymore; I could read and would in future just read the papers. Outside of school, I sang in the choir at church, read the lesson from the lectern and, when I was older, I carried the cross up the aisle at weddings or at Sunday service. I had a go at bell ringing but timing and co-ordination were not my thing. You could tell when I was in the bell tower; the peel sounded like a strangled cat in the parish of St Stephens.

After primary school, I moved to Wearde Comprehensive. I could not see what the big fuss was all about. As far as I was concerned, I just made the transition and got on with it. To me it was just more subjects structured with individual lessons, different teachers and a timetable. I enjoyed English and drama and playing rugby. I was a prop forward, right in the thick of it. During weekends and holidays I worked on a farm. I loved being outdoors, working with animals and helping bring in the harvests. It was also earning me some pocket money.

The first three years of secondary education did not faze me but when it came to picking my GCSE subjects, my interest started to wane. I began gazing out of the window, daydreaming across Mount Edgecombe, Antony Passage and Ince Estates. Apart from English and drama, the rest bored me. Of course, I knew education was important but my enthusiasm had gone.

What baffled me was my geography teacher moaning about having no money, after going all the way to Australia for an Easter break. Our family holidays were spent in caravans, converted barns or cottages on farms in Cornwall. Farming was seeing a major transformation from the conventional ways. Having to diversify to earn a living, many farms started offering bed and breakfast. I loved going on holiday to different farms to see how they worked. To this day, I am a firm supporter of Britain continuing farming. Too much land is being taken over for housing or out-of-town retail sites. We will never get that land back and far too much food is imported. Britain has an ideal mild climate for farming and needs to get back to producing more food again. Good land should not be used for wind farms and solar energy. Rows and rows of solar panels just look like sunglasses glaring from a distance. What a blot on the landscape.

My parents could not afford to go abroad. My father was the main breadwinner in the house and it wasn't until my brother and I were both in secondary school that my mother started working as a playground assistant. We ate our evening meals together around the table, discussing our day. We were not allowed to leave the table until everybody had finished. They strongly believed in family values, though they did not always do or have what they wanted. Sacrifices were made for the benefit of the family.

Our last family holiday was spent in Jersey in the Channel Islands. I considered it to be abroad as it entailed a short aeroplane flight. While there, we went to Fort Regent, in St Helier, a family amusement park. I was given some time to go and do my own thing. Not being content with what was inside, I took the cable car down the cliff outside the park. I knew I should not be doing this but the rides inside the park were not enough for me. I had to go that one step further and get myself stranded outside. Without a ticket and very little money, I found myself stuck. We were in a world of no mobile phones, so, with puppy-dog eyes and a sorrowful face, I begged for money from strangers to get me back into the park. Whether this was my naivety or my adventurous spirit shining through, I'm not sure. What I got was a very stern look from my mother when we regrouped. To say she was not amused was an understatement.

Truth be told, I was starting to think beyond education to a career and earning a living. I had a vision of building my own house in the country when I started working. I never envisaged moving away but I did see myself doing something outside. I could not see myself working indoors, tied to an office or a machine. It needed to be a career that involved moving around. I always felt I could work with others but not necessarily with a supervisor or manager hanging over me. My parents never stood in the way of me doing what I wanted and it was clear that further education was not an option for me. I explored farm work, spending a week on a taster course at Duchy Agricultural College, Callington. As I had experience working with cattle, I showed a keen interest in the dairy industry. At the time, all I envisaged was milking a herd and working the land. In hindsight, I am so glad I never took that career option. What upheaval the dairy industry has seen – small family farms selling up or bought to form bigger corporations; competition from the ever-growing supermarkets and falling milk prices. If I had been a farm labourer, do you think I would have travelled and climbed the mountains I have? The average farm labourer does not earn very much relative to the hours they put in. I was also interested in the Forestry Commission but I could not start until I was twenty-one and I suffered with hay fever and eczema.

Leaving school in the summer of 1989, I immediately started work at Royal Mail as a Postal Cadet. Back then, Youth Training Schemes (Y.T.S.) were all the rage. I earned twenty-nine pounds a week in my first year and thirty-five in my second year. At the end of the second year, some employees were laid off so that the firm could recruit cheap labour. I was keen for a career and stability which Royal Mail gave me, keeping me on at the end of two years. To start with I walked the streets near where I live now six days a week. Now-adays I would have been classed as 'clinically obese' when I left school so walking and cycling six days a week was quite a shock to the system. I found that I lost weight quite rapidly needing alterations to my uniform in just a few months. By the second year, I had learnt to drive and I had a car, making life a lot easier. When I was transferred to Pennycomequick, Plymouth, I learned a lot more about Royal Mail and I began shift work, on a six-week rotation. I took regular stick for being from Cornwall. Cornish people have a reputation for being careful with their money. My usual reply was, 'It's great to be earning a living in Devon and taking it back to God's country to spend.'

I went out with a core group of mates from school, usually ending up in Plymouth or over at the Harbour Lights nightclub in Torpoint, Cornwall. For the next ten years, I went on lads' holidays to Florida and the Balearic and Canary Islands. Going abroad properly was a whole new experience for me. I enjoyed sampling different cultures and lifestyles. I certainly wasn't on the lookout for the nearest English pub or typical British food.

My first holiday was to Tenerife on a time share. Unfortunately it was double booked and saw the four of us lined up in front of a rather large Spanish man to sort the problem out. He reminded me of Jethro the charismatic Cornish comedian. I have travelled all over the world since this incident so I do not think it left too many scars. While we were there, we booked an excursion up Mount Teide. However, I had encouraged everybody to party hard until 3 a.m. the morning before, so we overslept and missed the excursion. I kept a very low profile the next day. Maybe I'll revisit that one again sometime.

I had joined Landrake Young Farmers Club, meeting at Geffrey Hall every Tuesday night. I was an active member for twelve years, playing sports, speaking publicly, performing in plays and taking part in competitions against other clubs in Cornwall. I would listen to Ian Davey speak, mesmerised by his ability to improvise and engage an audience without a prepared script. A group of young lads would pile into the back of a Sherpa van on mattresses and end up in Newquay or Truro for the night (they had a designated driver each time, I hasten to add). With all the red tape and legislation, would they get away with it now? I think not.

I took on the role of club secretary and treasurer. It was a great opportunity, not only to look after my own money, but to be trusted with the wider responsibility of looking after the club's finances. I took the job seriously and diligently chased people for membership subscriptions and late payments. My persistence in chasing, 'hard up' farmers for money paid dividends in the end. When I came to leaving Young Farmers, at the age of twenty-six, most people I knew were settling down and having families. But this hadn't happened for me, I wasn't ready. I was still keen to experience more of life.

I fractured my right foot while playing football on astro turf. I was lying on the couch watching television and eating chocolate digestives, piling on the pounds and feeling sorry for myself when *Wish You Were Here* came on. Martin Roberts was joining a trek up Kilimanjaro and talking through his journey to the summit. I was mesmerised, studiously taking in what was going on. It appealed to me and I thought it would be a fantastic way to get motivated again.

CHAPTER 3

ACONCAGUA 2001

The mountain's biggest blows are known as the
Viento Blanco and through the years they have
steadily filled a cemetery full of victims.

— DAVID KEATON

Once I had got over the exhaustion and euphoria of what I had just achieved, I was keen for more. During my Kilimanjaro expedition I met Paul, whom I shared a tent with, and Vince and Ben. We formed a nice team and subsequently went on a few trips together. Ben was young and boisterous but he was also keen and enthusiastic. Paul, Vince and I were more cautious in our approach. Ben was keen to tackle Aconcagua, a totally different proposition to Kilimanjaro, being higher and therefore, more physically demanding. He not only wanted us to climb Aconcagua, but also organise the trip ourselves. I did not want the extra pressure and responsibility, preferring to pay for an expert's knowledge of the area. Vince countered that we all needed more experience, which pacified Ben for a few months and gave us time to get to know each other as friends and climbing partners.

A week's winter mountaineering in Glen Coe, Scotland, in January 2000, was an eye opener for me. It was nowhere near as high as Kilimanjaro or Aconcagua but it threw up climatic conditions of a different nature.

The wind and rain were extremely unpleasant and made the air feel colder than it actually was. We spent the days walking in crampons and digging snow holes in case we needed to shelter from bad weather or be under-cover in an emergency. We learnt how to ice-axe arrest, which would become invaluable to me in years to come. When orienteering across Aonach Mor one fog-bound, wet day, I had a chastening experience. My hands had become so cold that I had lost all feeling in them. What was I going to do? How could I expect to survive on a mountain just short of 7,000 metres when I was struggling at 1,000 metres?

By the end of the week, we were knackered but warm after sampling Scotland's finest whiskies. We reviewed the week's climb and, several whiskies later, we all agreed to holiday in the Alps during the summer to climb Mont Blanc and improve our skills. Before then, I needed to buy some better equipment, including gloves and a warmer coat to go under my Gore-Tex.

At 4,807 metres, Mont Blanc is the highest mountain in the Alps and generally takes most of the bad weather, while the peaks behind are fine. Sure enough, terrible weather is what we got for a week in July 2000. We stayed in the pretty, quiet village of Megève, just outside Chamonix, which is a magnet for climbers, skiers and snowboarders. It offers a wide range of outdoor shops, restaurants and bars and is renowned for its nightlife. There I made some expensive purchases, including a down sleeping bag and down coat, suitable for conditions below minus twenty-five. At the time, the availability of these items in Britain was scarce. An additional incentive was the tax savings to be made before the Euro came.

We had an atrocious week of weather. Every time we went out, we got soaked. However, we did manage to do some acclimatisation walks, so we decided it was worth hiring two guides and attempting to reach the summit. Normally the walk between Le Nid d'Aigle and Refuge du Goûter, at 3,817 metres, takes four to six hours but in the bad weather, it took a lot longer. Trudging uphill in knee-high snow was energy sapping. During the week, through lack of good weather, not enough climbing at altitude had been done. We were not acclimatised and the conditions were hard. Reaching the Refuge du Goûter a lot later than planned meant we only had a short while to rest before attempting the summit, a further 1,000 metres up. The guide said I did well to attempt it, but I eventually turned back as the conditions got worse. Thigh-deep snow was the sort of thing I expected in the winter, not the summer. My core had got cold while I was being helped into my spare fleece. I knew this was not mine and Vince's day. Paul and Ben walked a bit further on but they eventually turned back too. Vince later said it would have been foolhardy to have carried on. Turning back was the right decision. Weary and exhausted, we made our way back down; Mont Blanc would wait for another day.

Much to Ben's dismay, I decided to climb Aconcagua with an organised company. I had little knowledge or experience of the mountains but I was still up for the challenge. Aconcagua is a serious undertaking and it could fill a cemetery with the number of victims it has claimed. Aconcagua, in South America, is the highest mountain in the southern hemisphere and second highest of the seven summits at 6,962 metres. The Seven Summits Challenge is the quest to reach the highest point on each continent. Climbing them all has become one of the most sought after achievements in modern mountaineering. Aconcagua would be a far greater test of my prowess than Kilimanjaro.

The name 'Aconcagua' comes from the word 'Quechua' from the Inca language, meaning 'stone sentinel'. It is part of the Andes which is the longest mountain range in the world at over 7,000 kilometres long. They comprise continuous waves of peaks from the shores of the Caribbean in the north to Cape Horn in Chile, in the south. Technically, Aconcagua lies to the east of the main Andean chain, in the smaller Frontal Range just inside Argentina's border with Chile. This is a barren region where snowfall is comparatively light. Aconcagua is not blessed with the spectacular corniced ridges and fluted ice faces that make up other South American mountains.

Aconcagua is shaped like a wedge. The gentle slope faces north-west, ending at an enormous col known as Nido de Condor (the Condor's Nest). This col can be gained from the Horcones valley to the west, or the Vacas valley to the east. This provides the easiest route up the mountain. The rocky West Face of Aconcagua is a huge expanse of loose gullies and buttresses, which are no good for climbing but are a splendid sight when bathed in the red light of the setting sun. The east side is much colder and the large Polish Glacier flows down sharply from near the top of the South-East Ridge. The steep side of the wedge is the colossal South Face, a 2,400-metre wall of rock and ice, which is capped by Aconcagua's wind-beaten North and South Summits.

Aconcagua can be mistaken for an eroded volcano but it is actually formed from built-up layers of volcanic sediments which were thrust up when the Andes were formed. Interestingly, the relatively close proximity of Aconcagua to the Chilean Trench in the Pacific Ocean creates the biggest 'wrinkle' in the face of the Earth, with a significant difference in altitude amounting to almost 14,000 metres. The best months for climbing Aconcagua are December to March, though November has become an increasingly popular time to climb. During the winter months, from May to August, most of the area is covered in snow and is extremely windy. At certain times the road between Santiago, Chile and Mendoza becomes impassable due to the major snowstorms and their effects on the roads. Even during the finest months, from December to February, the wind can be extreme above 5,000 metres. It is not uncommon to see a big lenticular cloud around the summit, indicating extremely high winds. This weather is known as the Viento Blanco (White Wind) and a summit attempt is extremely dangerous and nearly impossible under such circumstances. Viento Blanco has been known to blow for days on end.

The arid climate in the area makes the valleys leading up to Aconcagua look barren and desolate. In the lower areas, below 2,500 metres, only hardy bushes and grasses are found. Few areas have any trees and these are usually eucalypti planted by man. Wildlife is similarly sparse but if you're lucky you may see alpaca, a smaller cousin of the llama. Mountain lions are present but are rarely seen. Birds are rare but the sudden flutter of a hummingbird is quite common. Above 4,000 metres, the area is almost devoid of any kind of life and the environment is desert-like. There are smaller, camouflaged flowers which resemble small rocks, which are an amazing example of a species adapting to a tough climate.

The Inca Indians started exploring the high Andes long before Columbus discovered the New World. Artefacts have been found in remarkably high places, the highest being the summit of Llullaillaco. This mountain is a few hundred kilometres north of Aconcagua and rises to 6,739 metres. On Aconcagua itself, the skeleton of a guanaco (wild animal related to the llama) was found on the ridge connecting the North and South Summits. It is unlikely that a guanaco would have climbed there by itself but there is no evidence that indicates the Incas were responsible for its demise. A mummy was found in 1985 on one of Aconcagua's outlying peaks, at an altitude of 5,200 metres. Although there is no evidence that the Inca Indians climbed to the summit, it is possible they did, hundreds of years before the first recorded ascent.

In the early nineteenth century, the area was visited on many occasions. The first serious attempt to climb the mountain was in 1883 by a well-known alpinist Paul Gussfeldt who approached it from the Chilean side.

A determined attempt, he reached 6,450 metres on the North-West Ridge. In 1896, an expedition, led by the Englishman, Edward Fitzgerald, camped at the head of the Horcones Valley close to today's Base Camp for the Normal Route. Stuart Vines, another English climber, joined him along with several Swiss guides including Mathias Zurbriggen. After weeks of building camps and moving up the northwestern slopes, Matthias managed to summit alone on the fourteenth of January 1897. Other members of the expedition reached the summit a month later though not Fitzgerald himself.

The next notable ascent was made in 1934 by a group of Polish climbers. On the ninth of March, four of them climbed the glacier on the upper part of the East Face. Despite the wind and the low temperatures, they reached the summit from a camp at 6,300 metres. The whole climb was done alpine-style without any fixed camps. This route is now known as the Polish Glacier.

In the 1950s, climbers turned their attention to the impressive South Face. This incredibly high face is both difficult and dangerous with steep loose rock between ice cliffs and glaciers, layered like an unstable birthday cake. As Aconcagua is in the southern hemisphere, the South Face receives little sunshine, like a north face in the Alps or Himalaya. In 1953, the western boundary of the South Face, the long South West Ridge, was climbed. A year later, a French expedition, led by René Ferlet, established a Base Camp on the Inferior Horcones Glacier below the South Face. After a month of preparation, six climbers reached the summit taking a line up the right side of the face. Several climbs have been made up the South Face since, including Reinhold Messner's direct finish to the original French Route.

There are three approaches: the Normal, the Polish Glacier and the South Face routes. Each taking two to three days from the main road to

Base Camp. This is where all the routes on the mountain start. From Puente del Inca (on the Santiago-Mendoza road), through the Horcones Valley, one route leads to the Plaza del Mulas Base Camp, at 4,230 metres, and the start of the Normal Route, on the north-west side of the mountain. A right turn up the Lower Horcones Valley leads to Plaza Francia. This is the Base Camp used for the South Face. The approach to the east side of the mountain starts from Punta de Vacas, approximately fifteen kilometres from Puente del Inca on the road to Mendoza. The Base Camp, Plaza Argentina, can be reached from the Vacas Valley and Relinches Valley. Nearly 3,000 climbers a year attempt Aconcagua but the success rate is less than fifty per cent. Most climbers follow the North West Ridge from the Horcones Valley, which offers the best chance of success. Consequently, the camps are crowded in the height of the season (December and January). Base Camp is manned by a doctor and there is a hotel a short walk away. Climbers must register with the Aconcagua National Park and pay a fee. Though the summit can be reached in three days from Base Camp, it is not recommended. Climbers should allow a week to adapt to the altitude before making an attempt.

The management of Aconcagua's environment has undergone a tremendous transformation over the last twenty-five years. Previously termed a 'dirty' mountain, with litter blanketing the trails and camp sites, it is now clean and well cared for through a simple but effective waste-management programme. The Park Authorities give every visitor a rubbish bag when they enter the park. If the bag is not full at the end of a trip, the visitor is fined on the spot. Toilet facilities are also being developed and placed around the Base Camps of the two major approach routes, in an effort to solve the growing sanitation problem.

From around 6,000 metres, the east route can be climbed in one day. A more direct version has also been climbed: the South Face French

Route takes the central spur of the Face. It involves mixed climbing on far-from-perfect rock and in steep snow to reach the South East Ridge to the summit. The 1974 Messner variation is often used, finishing at the ridge between the South and North Summits. We climbed the Normal Route, the most popular route on the mountain. It poses few technical challenges apart from the altitude and weather. Two or three camps are used on the way. The final section of the climb is a steep scree-filled gully, the notorious Canaleta.

I travelled with Inka Expediciones, which is based in Mendoza, Argentina. The leader was a young man with very little expedition experience but he did come from the region, which was to prove crucial. The cost price of the trip was about the same as Kilimanjaro, plus two weeks' annual leave. However, I did need to invest in more equipment like mountaineering boots, crampons and gloves to try and cope with the cold and the high winds.

I met the team in Mendoza, between Christmas and New Year. When we were in Buenos Aires, in transit to Mendoza, I again witnessed poverty on a scale not found in Cornwall. While we were eating a meal at a table outside, children came up to me begging for food or money. Their parents were standing a few metres away, urging them to come over. It made me appreciate how fortunate I am. I noticed some people driving old Cortinas and Escorts. It was like going back to the early eighties in England.

Just like on Kilimanjaro, we comprised an international team, although, this time, much younger and closer in age. I knew that one team member at least, a Welshman, would, like myself, find the heat in the valley hard to bear as, in Wales and Cornwall, we are just not used to heat and humidity in the mid-thirties. Our counterparts from Brazil and Peru soaked up the sun and adapted much better to the climate. After introducing myself to everybody, I realised that I had the least mountaineering experience.

Some of my colleagues had climbed in the Himalaya and South America. My efforts on Kilimanjaro paled into insignificance by comparison. Not easily fazed, I approached the expedition with an open mind. We all have to start somewhere, that's how we gain experience.

To get on the mountain, we went via the Horcones Valley. This meant walking in a basin in forty-degree heat. The heat was what I was most fearful of. Covering up my head and wearing a loose, long-sleeved top I made my way slowly up the valley with just a small rucksack. The bulk of my equipment was on mules inside my massive North Face duffle bag. Plaza de Mulas was Base Camp, at 4,250 metres. From there, I could see a mass of tents from other expeditions, the resident doctors and the hotel. It meant the end of the line for the mules. They would not go any further up the Normal Route. It also meant that unless we paid for a personal Sherpa, we would have to carry our own belongings in a rucksack; only I did not have a large rucksack and my duffle bag was not designed to carry large loads. I had made a fundamental mistake in not following the kit list. By my own stupidity, I had made my assault on Aconcagua a whole lot harder. Now I was carrying the duffle vertically on my back, the weight naturally fell to the bottom, which put more pressure on my waist and hips, tiring and straining them. I was also carrying a share of the team's gear and food. Hiring a Sherpa was not an option for me. Seeing how well I coped carrying the load was part of the challenge. I considered myself to be strong, but how strong was I at high altitude?

After a couple of days' rest, we made a first carry to Camp 1 at 5,000 metres. We had already lost a Brazilian man from the team. He had received a call informing him that his father had been taken ill. He was obviously disappointed that his trip had been curtailed so we commiserated with him and wished him well. The mountains will always be there but the same cannot be said of family. The rest of us carried on. It was a slow, hard, hot and humid slog to Camp 1, in plastic boots, without any crampons, in arid conditions. By the time we came back down, we were knackered. It was the first time I had ever carried anything in these conditions. No gym or hill-walking in Cornwall could prepare me for this. We adopted the same philosophy as when we were on Kilimanjaro, walking high and recovering lower down in order to acclimatise quicker. Our strategy proved successful and by the time I went to Camp 1, I felt stronger and faster. Resting is important in mountaineering. Replenishing the body with food and fluid is essential. Increased sweating through the lungs, which rapidly fill with dry air and absorb the body's moisture, causes dehydration at high altitude.

As we rested back down at Base Camp, we regularly heard the noise of a rescue helicopter coming to the aid of a stricken climber. When signing up for these expeditions, helicopter repatriation is the part of the insurance a climber hopes to never use. The helicopters reminded us of our hazardous nature of our surroundings. Most international guides have lost a friend or colleague through mountaineering. At Condors Nest (Camp 2, 5,400 metres) we experienced very strong winds because our camp was very exposed. It was important that we communicated clearly while performing camp duties, such as erecting tents, because the loss of tents and equipment in high winds means, quite simply, the end of the trip. It is important to keep drinking water on rest days, between moving to higher camps, because dehydration can lead to lethargy.

The more experienced Welsh guy was quicker than me. He was leaner and had experienced this altitude before. Moving to Berlin, Camp 3, at 6,000 metres, was, again, slow and hard. The altitude was new territory for me – by comparison Kilimanjaro is 5,895 metres. You may think that 6,000 metres is not very far, but when you consider the pressure the altitude puts on the body, not to mention the humidity, the buffeting winds and the weight of the load, to succeed is a great achievement. From Berlin Camp, we made our summit attempt.

We reached the peak in very high winds. In fact, we were in the middle of a Viento Bianco storm. This was exactly what I had read about before my trip, gusts of fifty to sixty miles per hour, plus temperatures of minus twenty-two degrees, which made the environment very inhospitable indeed. The hands suffer the most because we need them to be able to do anything – work zippers, tie knots and prepare camps. Gusts whipping across exposed planes threatened to deny us of our hats and gloves. We had to make sure we held on to everything tightly. Everybody was evacuating from other expeditions, high-tailing it down the mountain, but our young leader said we would stay a while and see if the wind dropped. Nobody queried or questioned his judgement call. I went to bed, after I had eaten some food, with a cracking headache.

When we awoke the next day, the weather was a lot better and the wind had dropped. This was why I paid to travel with a local company. Had I attempted Aconcagua on my own, I may have descended with the other climbers. The leader's decision to stay had been a good one. That night we would go for the summit. We spent the rest of the day taking on fluid and preparing ourselves. We checked our cameras and gear and put fresh batteries in our head torches. When I woke up, my adrenaline was pumping and I felt good to go for the summit – I had summit fever, that same buzz of anticipation I felt just before I climbed the final leg of Kilimanjaro. However, I knew that this time the journey would be a lot harder because I was sore and tired from load carrying. I chose not to eat or drink very much and I started off fine. The weather was good and it did not seem very cold. I felt as though I did not need the down jacket I was wearing but, later on, I came into some difficulty. Lack of food and fluid, combined with the rigour of the mountain, were taking their toll. Feeling good earlier had been a fallacy. I was battling with altitude sickness.

There are two types of high altitude sickness: HACE and HAPE. High Altitude Cerebral oedema (HACE) is the swelling of the brain, caused by fluid retention in the brain tissue. Those afflicted slur their words and walk as though they are drunk. High Altitude Pulmonary oedema (HAPE) is when the lungs fill up with fluid and the heart becomes pressurised, which can cause a person to drown in their own fluids. Both these illnesses can prove fatal and the best way of dealing with them is to descend. I was showing signs of HACE. The guide gave me some medication and I kept on going. My awareness was still good and I was not stumbling with every step, just occasionally. My colleagues, who had already summited, spoke words of encouragement as they passed me on their way down the mountain, though I was almost oblivious to what they said. It was just as though I was drunk. As a person drinks more, they become less co-ordinated and responsive. Altitude sickness is similar but with dire consequences. I made it to the summit through sheer determination, because I was too stubborn to give up. As the medication kicked in, I started to feel better. My photographs show me looking rough, suffering from acute mountain sickness, dehydration and lack of food. The feeling of elation was not there, I was almost unaware of where I was, standing by the summit cross, hungover and swaying slightly. I looked around at the surrounding Andes in my own little world. Even though Aconcagua was arid and desolate, the views from the summit should have been awe-inspiring but I couldn't appreciate them considering how I was feeling.

I was slow coming down, which was not altogether to do with the effects of altitude. I was conscious of putting pressure on my knees, so I tried to look after them. The wide but steep scree paths played havoc with them so I preferred to take my time. I also like to look around. We spent so much time going up, why not indulge in the views on the way back down? At Berlin, I got a huge cheer from my comrades who had all summited. In the coming days, we would pack up and make our way down the mountain to Mendoza. It was then that I became acutely aware of the smell radiating from everybody. The aroma of sweat, dirt and dust was strong, after being in the same clothes for nearly two weeks. Our clothing protected our bodies from the sun's strong ultra violet rays but our exposed hands and faces were sunburnt. When I stripped off, I looked like a beacon. Showers and clean clothes were very welcome indeed.

After having celebratory drinks in Mendoza and saying my goodbyes, I was, again, looking forward to being at home in Cornwall – my home and sanctuary, where I liked to reflect while walking along the coast and moorlands. It was time to go back to civvy street, to work and routine. I was obviously chuffed I had climbed the second highest of the seven summits but it had been far more difficult than Kilimanjaro with the physical battering I had received from carrying the loads. I had learnt a valuable lesson, to read the kit list carefully. That duffle bag has been relegated to the loft. I have never used it since, except as storage, but I keep it as a reminder. I coped with extreme changes in temperature from forty degrees in the valley, to minus twenty-two, with fifty- to sixty-mile-per-hour winds, at 6,000 metres. It was hard but I came through it. Discipline is key on a mountain. If I were to go any higher, I needed to learn a few things – loss of appetite, dehydration from not drinking and acute mountain sickness would need to be addressed. The use of Diamox and its values would have to be considered. Strength comes from the mind as well as the body.

CHAPTER 4

BREAKING DOWN ON A SUMMIT

The uncontrollable emotion just poured out of me.
It had been a tough few months prior to the trip.

— ED BUCKINGHAM

Between Aconcagua and my next adventure, I moved house for the second time to a property just down the road in Saltash. I saw the move as a progression up the property ladder as I was upsizing from a one-bedroom terrace to a two-bedroom semi-detached. I have always considered Saltash to be an ideal commute to work and it is a short distance from the coast and moors. Although I had found this new passion for adventure, I considered it a hobby, not a career opportunity. My stability and future was with Royal Mail, even though it was coming under the ever increasing pressure of privatisation. In comparison to the other six summits, my next adventure was right on my doorstep – Elbrus (5,642 metres), in Russia.

When Mikhail Gorbachev launched his political reformation programmes, *perestroika* and *glasnost*, it allowed unrestricted access to the Caucasus and its mountain range, ending more than seventy years of semi-isolation. Squeezed between the Black and Caspian seas, the Caucasus range is nearly 1,500 kilometres long and 130 kilometres wide. It contains fourteen mountains higher than Mont Blanc (which rises to 4,807 metres). One hundred of the mountains are above 4,000 metres. The height of the Caucasus accounts for the range's considerable snow cover. There are many glaciers and crevasses, which can be a problem. The glaciers on Elbrus are generally smaller than those found in the Alps. Elbrus looks distinctly different from the other Caucasus mountains – a massive two-headed volcano plastered in ice. It is covered by glaciers both large and small, which are hundreds of metres thick in places. The peak has been described as 'little Antarctica'.

The Caucasus is the borderline between Europe and Asia, and includes south-east Russia, Armenia, Azerbaijan and Georgia. With one of the highest concentrations of separatist territories, the region is fraught with violent conflict. During the trip, I carried my passport at all times as there were regular border patrols. Civil unrest continues most notably in Chechnya, which has been in conflict with Russia since 1785 and still remains politically unstable. While accessing the Caucasus from Georgia, in the south, remains difficult, Elbrus and the high mountains of the Central Caucasus can normally be easily and safely accessed from Russia in the north.

Though at a similar latitude to the Pyrenees, the climate of the Caucasus is very different. The Black and Caspian seas have a huge effect on the climate and precipitation. To the north is the Russian Steppe and beyond the forest steppe and the Arctic Circle. In the south is the desert and semi-desert of the Middle East and Arabia. Nestled between are the forest and alpine pastures of the High Caucasus. Whereas the southern slopes are very dry and sub-tropical, the northern slopes are much cooler. Temperatures fall very quickly above the treeline and snowline. The Caucasus mountains are much higher than the Alps so it rarely rises above freezing. Even in the summer nights, it can fall to below minus eight degrees, providing excellent snow and ice conditions. Above the snowline, even during the day, minus thirty degree temperatures have been recorded, making it very treacherous. Although July and August offer the most stable weather, afternoon thunderstorms are frequent and longer periods of heavy rainfall and snowfall do occur. Elbrus is notorious for its cold and violent winds and sudden weather changes, and the peaks offer little shelter from the elements. Its icy wastes make disorientation a very real danger in poor visibility. Once off the main trail, the glacier is littered with deep crevasses.

In technical climbing terms, Elbrus is a straightforward ascent on moderately angled snow and ice. However the weather, altitude and demands on stamina prevent many from reaching the summit. There is only one climbing route on the West Peak (the South-East Face) from inside Russia. From the barrel huts, a ninety-minute walk up the dry glacier leads to the site of the old Pruitt Refuge. A steady ascent passes Pastukhov Rocks at 4,700 metres. From there, the route climbs leftwards around the rocks of the East Peak and up into the massive snow basin between the West and East Peaks. Above the bivouac shelter on Sedlowina Saddle, the ascent leads up a steep snow and ice slope, past rocks to cross the horizontal ridge crest to the summit. It is also possible to ascend the West Peak via the South Face of the South-West Peak.

The flora and fauna on the mountain is similar to that found in the European Alps. Beyond the treeline, a wide variety of flowers and plants can be found, including several types of berries. The forest belt is known for its giant shrubs which are five times their standard height. Animals such as goats, ibex, chamois, golden eagles, wolves and bears are common. Surprisingly, the bears are shy and avoid confrontation, and the wolves are less intimidating than the wolfhounds used by shepherds to keep them away. Smaller predators such as lynx, wildcat and marten can sometimes be seen.

Elbrus can be climbed from most directions and the mountain's uniform nature has produced a variety of similar routes to the West Peak. Ease of access from the valley and decent accommodation have established the Azau approach as the most popular line of ascent. Reached from the village of Terskol in the upper Baksan Valley, there is easy access to a modern cable car and a less modern chair lift that takes climbers a good distance up the mountain. This used to leave a walk of an hour or so up the glacier to the refuge of the Eleven Hut, now known as the Pruitt. In the summer of 1991, the old refuge burnt down in a fire that killed a climber and injured others. There were about one hundred people inside at the time. It was built in the 1930s. The three-storey aluminium-clad hut was capable of sleeping up to two hundred climbers.

Briton, Chris Pearson was inside when the fire broke out: 'We got out, but there was someone banging at one of the windows on the top floor we had just come from. We tried to throw rocks to break the window and we gathered rucksacks together to form a landing cushion but the smoke was everywhere around us. After a while, we just had to leg it. We went up a few days later and all that was left was the remains of the caved-in aluminium shell and smouldering timbers. The walls had acted like an incinerator.'

Since the fire, climbers have been using half a dozen barrel-shaped huts, located at the top of the chair lift. Each hut sleeps six but accommodation is considerably smaller than the Pruitt. Although the cable car and chair lift gave easy access to Elbrus and allowed an acclimatised party to ascend to the huts, climb the mountain the next day and descend to the valley in twenty-four hours, this is dangerous for the non-acclimatised. The summit of Elbrus is 3,500 metres above Terskol and most climbers need four to six days' climbing and walking at increasing altitude to prepare to attempt the peak. Once most of the high mountains of the Alps had been climbed, Britain's Victorian mountaineers started to look further afield. Interest grew in the big unclimbed peaks of the Caucasus. Of the ten highest mountains in the range, nine were first climbed by members of the Alpine Club.

Russian climbers became more active on Elbrus in the 1930s and this continued into the early 1940s until the USSR was drawn into the Second World War. After the war, Russian climbers returned to the mountains, climbing many of the hard north faces and making spectacular traverses of the long, high ridges that are a feature of the Caucasus. Although there were many climbing clubs in the area foreign visitors found the bureaucracy daunting to overcome during the Cold War. The opening up of Russia in the 1980s changed everything and paved the way for an open and unrestricted Elbrus to take its rightful place in world mountaineering. Although the route up Elbrus is technically straightforward, it is a long day with little respite. It takes seven to nine hours from the huts to the saddle and a further one to two hours to the summit.

Kilimanjaro, at 5,895 metres, may be higher than Elbrus, but an ascent of Elbrus on a mediocre day with the wind blowing will give a clearer indication as to whether a person has the stamina to reach the higher seven summits. Elbrus and the Caucasus have a long history of human habitation and over one hundred years of mountain exploration and climbing. The area also has many good skiing resorts. During the Soviet era, the huts and the skiing and tourist facilities were well-maintained. Now that is no longer the case. Today, the mountain huts are badly managed and collection points for garbage and litter have been neglected. There are no plans to replace the famous Pruitt. With Elbrus' growing popularity, lack of accommodation on the mountain needs to be addressed soon. The site has become a garbage dump.

I attempted the summit in July 2002. This time of year offered the most stable weather. However, during the afternoons, thunderstorms and longer periods of heavy rain and snowfall were common. Elbrus is notorious for its cold, violent wind and sudden changes in weather, and it offers little protection from the elements. In technical climbing terms, Elbrus is straightforward on moderately angled snow and ice. The mountain is part of a national park but the authorities are not adequately funded to manage waste disposal. Instead, climbers, guides and tourist operators are asked to take out their waste and tread lightly, to minimise impact on the area. Weather, altitude and lack of stamina prevent many from reaching the summit.

I met up with four other international clients in Moscow on a nine-day trip. As I was only travelling as far as Russia, I did not suffer the jetlag I experienced in Tanzania and Argentina and I wanted to explore. Spending a few hours in the city, I had the chance to do some sightseeing. I saw the mosques and the Kremlin Wall. Just off Red Square, I went into a park where I got myself into a bit of trouble. Happily snapping away with my camera, I got a shot of a policeman on horseback. He moved briskly towards me, wagging his finger, like a wiper blade on a car and warned that under no circumstances can pictures be taken of the law in Russia. Unlike Mrs Ruse at primary school, he could not send me outside, he just issued a stern warning, telling me not to do it again. That was enough sightseeing for me; it was time to get on the mountain.

Meeting the other climbers, I found that the chemistry between us was lacking, compared with the Kilimanjaro team. It was as if we had all turned up as individuals to get the job done, climb the mountain and then go our separate ways again. Andrea Capussela was Italian and had a PhD in cross-border aspects of competition law. Until 2008, he worked on mergers and acquisitions. Then he moved to Kosovo where, until the end of March, he was the head of the economics unit of the International Civilian Office. Max Bleyleben was from Munich, but he was working in the United Kingdom. Max was an investment director at Kennet, a London-based growth equity investor in technology companies in Europe and the United States. At Kennet, Max oversaw the firm's interest in several technology companies including trading partners, Spreadshirt, NTRglobal, Tele-medicine Clinic and FRSGlobal. He authors a blog called 'Technofile Europe' that covers technology trends, entrepreneurship and venture capital, among other topics. Alessandro Balp was also Italian and worked in Milan. He was a partner at the Bonelli Erede Pappalardo, Yale Law School. Dealing with all areas of law, he had established a good reputation and was respected within his fraternity. Ben Grass was a fellow Brit and managing director of Pure Grass Films. He produced *Beyond the Race* (MySpace's first series, outside the US) and executive produced *Kirill* (MSN's first online series, outside the US which won a Webby for Best Drama Episode in 2009). He was formerly responsible for Sony Pictures Digital in Europe and prior to that was senior advisor, corporate strategy at the BBC. He held a degree in modern history from Oxford and an MBA from INSCAD. The group I was with was made up of truly professional people. I had always considered myself to have done well but I was feeling inferior among these people. Being a postman had served me well up to now, but, for somebody who has drive and determination, I was feeling like I had stayed very much within my comfort zone.

From Moscow we flew to Mineralnye Vody, a spa town, north of the Caucasus. In Abau Aln, we picked up our local Russian guide and leader, Viktor Lanchenko. He was a big man with broad shoulders. He was a lot older than the guides on Kilimanjaro and Aconcagua and he came across as being brusque and unfriendly. In the Baksan Valley a cable car took us up to the Garabashi (barrel) huts, at 3,850 metres. From there we hiked up the alpine valley to the newly named Pruitt Refuge, at 4,200 metres. The remains of the old Pruitt Refuge were still there. This would be our base for the remainder of the trip.

Walking in mountaineering boots and crampons is a skill. We learned to walk with our feet apart so as not to spike ourselves or rip our clothing.

We did two acclimatisation walks up to Pastukhov Rocks but I felt this was not enough walking. The best prevention of altitude sickness is to ascend gradually and be alert to early signs of symptoms. A climber should limit the rate of between 300 and 600 metres per day. Alpine-style ascents should include a prolonged acclimatisation period of seven to ten days at 4,300 metres.

It was noisy sleeping in the huts at night. Even light snow made a noise on the galvanised roof. Inside, the huts were made of wood and the sound of walking and shutting dormitory doors reverberated around the walls. Lack of sleep had not put the group in the best frame of mind for climbing, I was not having the easiest expedition. Nevertheless, I did summit with Andrea Capussela, who was suffering a bit from too few acclimatisation walks. My reaction to summiting Elbrus was different from Kilimanjaro and Aconcagua. I broke down and sobbed profusely. At high altitude, emotions are exacerbated. Why was I crying now? The trip and climb had been nowhere near as arduous and debilitating as Aconcagua. Leading up to Elbrus, I had received news from home that my dad had been diag-nosed with heart disease. My family and I were shocked. I considered him to be fit, active and healthy, he grew fruit and vegetables on his allotment which were part of his staple diet. The main cause was stress and the fact that he had been bottling it up inside of him for years. He had just been dealing with the pressures of everyday life, taking on more and more responsibility and, added to this, he had high cholesterol. Changes would have to be made to his lifestyle, workload and diet if he were to enjoy life in future years. Privately, I was concerned about his reaction to this news and how he would deal with it. Help was on hand from family but, at the end of the day, it was down to him to look after himself. The emotional breakdown Andrea was witnessing was my release. I am not one to show emotion, preferring to do it in private. No matter what comforting words

Andrea used or how much shoulder patting he did, he could not stop me sobbing. Given a little time, I did compose myself and descended.

On our way down to the hut, I was walking slowly at the back, practising my John Wayne-inspired duck walk (bending the knees and bouncing slightly). I was being careful not to catch my clothing on a rogue crampon, which may have sent me sprawling. The walk is tiring on the hips but it preserves the knees. Viktor, our guide was behind me, almost cattle-prodding me down the mountain because he wanted to get back to the hut. I could not see the point because, although the weather was overcast, it was not overly windy and we could see the hut down in the distance, looming ever nearer. A leader should walk at the speed of the last client. The stubborn side of me came out and I deliberately walked slower, frustrating him even more. The Cornish side of me came out too. It is customary to tip the leader according to how good their service is and my money stayed firmly in my wallet.

Elbrus had given me a small insight into what I was to experience later during my 'Seven Summits Challenge'. The demands on stamina and altitude acclimatisation had made Elbrus difficult. I felt we had not done nearly enough preparation walks. Spending sufficient time at altitude increases the red blood cells and sends more oxygen around the body. Using Diamox helps but I did not take it on this trip. If I had tried to rush the process, I could have ended up getting into difficulties. There were several things running around inside my head. I wanted to raise money for the British Heart Foundation to help people like my father but, to my knowledge, not many people in Cornwall were conversant with my Seven Summits Challenge. What challenge could I do to raise money? Wouldn't it be great to be met by my family, after coming through the arrival halls following such a momentous expedition?

I was also concerned about my work and the increasing threat of privatisation. In the 1980s, under Margaret Thatcher, we lived in an era where large companies were coming into financial difficulty and being sold off and floated. The problem had escalated from the infamous miners' strikes and pit closures. Employees were being laid off and the few remaining were offered shares as an incentive for accepting their new terms of employment. As new governments came into power, it was obvious they were still in favour of privatisation. I did have an underlying feeling that privatisation would come to us eventually; it was just a case of when. One decision I had made was to come off the temporary manager roles I was fulfilling at work, on a 'if and when required basis'. One week I was working with my colleagues, the next I was managing them. With my father's situation to deal with, I did not want the extra stress and responsibility and, in the current climate of cost cutting, the axe would eventually come down on the excessive number of floor managers Royal Mail employs. Though I had found my passion in mountaineering, it is not the cheapest pastime and I had to balance this with my living costs at home. As the challenges got bigger, the costs became greater.

Returning to the tranquillity of Cornwall, I had completed another of the seven summits. Elbrus had brought out the emotional side of me but the trip had not been as arduous as Aconcagua or as enjoyable as Kilimanjaro. I needed a tougher challenge, one where I was required to carry loads and improve my mountaineering skills of crampon walking and using an ice-axe, rather than just using it as a leaning post or pointer.

CHAPTER 5

ALASKA

*The secret of success on McKinley is to ensure that you
are poised for the summit when the good weather arrives.*

— STEVE BELL

Soon after I returned home, I began to get itchy feet and, before long,
I had booked my next expedition. However, it was important that I didn't
channel all my energy into holidays. In early 2003, I made another move
up the housing ladder. At the time, property prices had risen and, combined with a double-dip recession, people were struggling to get the
money together to put a deposit down. Gone were the days where people
like me could afford to move in on their own. There was a growing trend
in couples or mates buying together.

Denali in Alaska was by far the most exciting and enjoyable trip I have
ever done but it was very expensive. Denali is the highest mountain in
North America and, behind Everest, it is the second most difficult climb
of the seven summits. Nestled between Foraker and Hunter, it towers
at 6,194 metres, presenting a tough challenge, camping out on snow and
icy glaciers. There are no mules or Sherpas to share the load so it was down
to me to carry and pull a sledge. It is impossible to replace the calories
burned while ascending Denali. Lying just south of the Arctic Circle, it is
one of the coldest mountains anywhere in the world. Because it is so

close to the Pole, the barometric pressure makes it comparable to a 7,000-metre peak in the Himalaya. Denali is at the apex of the Alaska Range, stretching from the Aleutian Peninsula, through central Alaska and curving south-east to meet the Mount St Elias Range in Canada. Denali has three major glaciers – Muldrow, Ruth and the Kahiltna, although seven large glaciers in all including the Peters and Harper. It has two summits, the South (6,194 metres) and the lower North (5,934 metres), separated by the Denali Pass. This wild region is 240 kilometres from Alaska's largest city, Anchorage. The closest town is Talkeetna, a forty-minute flight away. The native Inuit people called the mountain Denali, meaning 'The High One'. It was in 1896 that it was given the name McKinley, after the then presidential candidate William McKinley. In more recent years, both the mountain and the national park it resides within are usually referred to as Denali it is the mountain with two names, but I can assure you I have only climbed it once.

The weather in Alaska is notorious for changing dramatically. The stable months are April to June, but April is cold, making May and June the most popular. July and August are very poor for climbing. Climbers must prepare themselves for stormbound days, when they will be confined to camp. It gets very cold. I had gained some experience of this on Aconcagua. The secret of success on Denali is to be prepared to summit when the good weather arrives. Wildlife and plants are almost non-existent on the higher peaks. There isn't much life above the snowline, but lower down animals such as moose, reindeer, bear and wolf can be seen and pesky mosquitoes abound.

The first serious attempt to climb Denali was in 1903. The expedition gave up below the Wickersham Wall, which is named after James Wickersham, the expedition's leader. A group led by Dr Frederick Cook first circumnavigated the peak in 1903. Three years later, Cook returned to climb Denali returning with a picture of himself flying the American flag from the 'summit'. Later the picture was found to be a fake. A few years later, a team of gold miners called 'Sourdoughs' made a bet they could climb Denali. Starting in December, they approached the mountain from the north with horses and dog sleds. On the third of April 1910, they set out and climbed the North Peak from their high camp in a gruelling eighteen-hour trip. They carried a large spruce-tree pole, which they planted on the summit rocks. Their pole was sighted by the first team to climb the main summit three years later.

Harry Karstens, a local guide, Walter Harper, Robert Tatum and Hudson Stuck, an Englishman, finally climbed the higher South Peak in 1913. In 1951, the West Buttress Route was pioneered by Bradford Washburn, Bill Hackett and Jim Gale. The name Bradford Washburn is inextricably linked with Denali because of his record keeping and photography. His crystal clear photographs of the mountain and other Alaskan peaks have provided a valuable source of information for a generation of mountaineers. In 1947, his wife Barbara became the first woman to stand on top of Denali. The massive South Buttress was first climbed in 1954 and the same team descended by the Muldrow Glacier to complete the first traverse of the mountain. In the late 1950s to early 1960s, attention turned towards the formidable 3,000-metre South Face, the steepest and highest face on the mountain. In 1959, the West Rib was climbed, this route starts below the South Face but climbs along its western edge. The renowned Italian climber Riccardo Cassin led an expedition in 1961 to the blunt ridge which divides the South Face. The team completed the climb despite facing difficulties never before encountered on Denali. The Cassin Ridge is perhaps the finest route on the mountain. With the ascent of the East Buttress in 1963, all the major flanks of the mountain were climbed with many new routes and variations discovered in the 1970s and 80s.

The first winter ascent of the mountain was made in February 1967 via the West Buttress Route. In 1970, Naomi Uemura became the first to climb Denali solo, using a bamboo pole tied to his waist to prevent him falling down crevasses. Returning in 1984, he made the first solo winter ascent. He reached the summit but got lost in a storm on the descent and his body was never found. Since 1980, Denali has increased in popularity and now attracts over 1,200 climbers a year. More than eighty per cent of these use the West Buttress route for its low level of difficulty and ease of access. All expeditions to the mountain must register in advance with the Denali National Park Service. Only six guiding companies are permitted to operate on Denali. They offer climbs up the West Buttress, the West Rib and Muldrow Glacier Routes.

We climbed the popular West Buttress Route. It starts from the South East Fork on the Kahiltna Glacier, where the plane dropped us off on the short ice runway, at 2,100 metres. From our Camp 3 at the Basin (4,330 metres up), the top of the West Buttress is reached. From the top camp, at 5,200 metres, the rising traverse to Denali Pass and the long climb over Archdeacon's Tower led to the summit. Of all the routes, litter and human waste are most commonly found along the West Buttress. The National Park Service on Denali is one of the best I have witnessed anywhere in the world. Climbers are given clear instruction to dispose of all litter and broken equipment and to throw human waste down deep crevasses. If caught doing otherwise, offenders are fined on the spot. The fines are big enough to deter any further attempts to break the rules. It's tough but it works. On more technical routes like the Cassin Ridge, abandoned equipment and fixed ropes are one of the major sources of litter. Occasional clean-ups by the National Park Service or volunteers remove much of it. As far as I am concerned, it is good to see. I am a firm believer in leaving a mountain as it was found. After all, I would not appreciate a guest defecating in my front room.

Up until now, my training for these expeditions had mainly consisted of joining the Caradon or Restormel Ramblers in Cornwall during their fourteen- to eighteen-mile walks. The Ramblers were predominantly older than me but I enjoyed their company. They were fascinated by my adventures. I also used to go swimming, which I have enjoyed since I was taught by an instructor at a young age but now I had to step up my training and it had to be cardio-vascular based. I could not afford to spend time training in the Alps so I had to make the best of my surroundings. I have never been a gym person, I find them claustrophobic and they remind me of the game *Mousetrap*. I prefer the outdoors and whatever the Cornish weather decides to throw at me. I find that being subjected to the weather elements helps me mentally prepare for the conditions I may encounter on a mountain. I began running twice a week on my own and I carried a rucksack weighing twenty-five kilograms, once a week, for five to eight hours, along steep inclines, to build up my stamina. There is no shortage of hills in Cornwall. I even walked in plastic boots. What a sight I must have looked going into cafes in Polperro for a bite to eat.

I met the rest of the team at *A Loon's Nest* Bed and Breakfast in Anchorage. There were eleven of us in total, comprising eight clients and three young, male guides. This was the first expedition our leader Ryan would undertake unsupervised. He was a big bear of a man, towering above everybody else. I was to see him carry far more than anybody else. As expedition leader, he also carried quite an extensive drugs case. He was accompanied by Clark and Bill. The first client I met was an American called Jim who proceeded to show me pictures of his frostbitten feet, from an abandoned trip the year before. Frostbite is a cold injury, usually localised, caused by the freezing of body tissue, which can die as a result of inadequate circulation. The first signs of frostbite are numbness, poor capillary refill and a white, waxy and wooden texture to the skin.

There are many factors contributing to frostbite – inadequate equipment, impatience and neglect. Most cases occur on days when a climber would have been better off staying within a tent, out of the cold, dry air. Convection heat loss dehydrates and exhausts climbers. On a summit day, a typical frostbite victim uses gloves instead of mittens, super gaiters instead of over-boots and ventures from camp in very high winds. I have never had a problem generating heat as I have always been a bit cuddly and my circulation has always been good. Jo and Rob Gambi were the only couple on the trip. Rob had been diagnosed with cancer for the second time, in 2000. They were at the start of an incredible journey that would eventually see them complete the seven summits in 2004. They had also planned to go to the North and South Poles and climb a host of other mountains during 2005. Their remarkable story was published in a book entitled *Holding On*. It was a privilege to meet them both.

Before we left Anchorage, our kit was given a thorough going over by the guides. All our bags were emptied and checked for equipment and clothes that would not be needed. They even cut our toothbrushes in half, which seemed quite unnecessary. Any purchases we needed were made at the massive REI store in Anchorage. I was advised to purchase plastic bottles and cutlery, which seemed odd to me at the time but I never questioned it. The next day we drove to Talkeetna to catch the flight on to the glacier.

After doing the preliminaries at the Denali National Park Service, it was time for the flight. The planes were only four-seaters so it took several trips to transport us and our gear on to the Kahiltna Glacier. I was lucky enough to be sitting up with the pilot in the cockpit. Unlike my brother, who had a tendency to fiddle when he was younger, I was very good and kept my hands firmly in my lap, not touching the buttons. The flight was wonderful and we travelled over forest and tundra and up to the mountains. This was the first time I appreciated the awesome scale of the Alaska Range.

Once we and our gear were on the glacier, we set up camp near the airstrip. I was sharing with Jack, who was sixty, from Wyoming. His gear looked as though it had come straight off the ark but he told me it was tried and tested. Privately, I wondered if the cold would get the better of him.

The next day, we carried the first cache up 2,440 metres to Ski Hill at the foot of Motorcycle Hill, at the North East Fork Junction. This would be our first day of pulling a sledge and carrying a load, which consisted of our clothing and food. We learnt to put the heaviest items near the top of the rucksack so as not to tire our hips pulling the sledge. Ryan encouraged us to take Diamox, half a tablet in the morning and half in the evening. I was happy to go along with his advice, bearing in mind my problems on Aconcagua, though I was wary of the side effects, remembering Liz on Kilimanjaro. At the end of the first day, Ryan produced a little black box and a notebook. He placed a pulse oximeter on our forefinger to measure the percentage of oxygen in our blood. At sea level, the reading should be between ninety-seven and ninety-nine per cent, but at altitude lower readings are to be expected. However, the readings are not always an accurate indication of a person's wellbeing. A climber can feel fine but have a low reading. Ryan monitored us regularly and stressed the importance of drinking lots of fluid and taking Diamox.

We ascended the mountain using ropes, connected between two or three of us and a guide. We were spaced equally apart and never let the rope go slack or tight. On glaciers, if somebody broke through thin ice we were relying on the other team members to react and grab the rope, stopping us falling further. On reaching the site of the next camp, we dug a very deep cache to prevent rooks from pilfering our food supplies. On filling the hole, we wanded the site and returned to camp. When climbers camp at a cache, it is turned into the kitchen tent and, therefore, serves two purposes. I now learnt why we were using plastic cutlery and bottles:

when it's severely cold, metal sticks to the tongue and lips, causing blisters that do not heal. Unfortunately, the next day, the weather was too bad for us to make any progress. With crevasses close by and poor visibility, it was too dangerous. We lost six days in total over the course of the trip, using up valuable food supplies. By the time we moved again, we had to break trail in fresh, deep snow. Not many jump at that prospect. So even though we had acclimatised, it was still hard work. Breakfast each morning was French toast, bagels and crispy bacon dripping with fat – heaven. I was not worried about my diet because I was burning calories during the days' exertions. It was impossible to eat the food to replace the calories. Bill then handed us a bag of snacks to ration over the course of the day. The route got steeper up the West Buttress and Motorcycle Hill, leading to the basin on Windy Corner at 3,960 metres. The days of carrying loads were hard with little respite. From time to time, we felt as though we had no privacy, even while taking a leak. I remember Jo shouting because she had to pee in front of the others. We were too near crevasses to unclip and wander off.

One day, good navigation by Bill and Clark got us into camp. Like thick fog, the weather had closed right in so I could barely see the person in front of me. It was an epic eleven-hour day. I was in my element though – yes it was new, living and travelling on snow, but the load carrying was right up my street. I was suffering no side effects from taking Diamox and I felt strong, thriving in the environment. Jack and I worked quite well together. I was obviously quicker while he was more slow and methodical. It reminded me of when I spent my childhood with Grandad.

We reached the only bit of technical climbing – a 240-metre headwall of forty-degree ice – which involved teamwork with a partner, keeping the rope tight and not allowing any slack. The first time we traversed this headwall was with the aim of making a cache at 4,998 metres. While I was climbing, I could feel the rope go slack. Clinging to the snow and ice like a limpet, I shouted down to Jack to pull the rope tight. It gave me an uneasy feeling. People can lose confidence very quickly, especially at high altitude. I found out later that he had let go of the rope because he felt his hand go cold. I told him that it was not to happen again and to concentrate on keeping warm and supporting his colleague, whether that was me or another team member. Upon reaching our destination, we discovered another cache which had obviously been left behind by a party the previous year who had been unable to retrieve it due to the appalling weather conditions. Consequently their cache had been left until now.

After making that cache, we were hit by some more bad weather. We fortified walls around the camp and kitchen tent. It was fun using a saw and cutting blocks out of the snow, like building with Lego. We never lay in our tent that long without being aware of the weather. Tents had to be free of snow to avoid suffocation. We did eventually move up the headwall and then up to 5,240 metres, where we made our last camp before the summit push. Again, we experienced more bad weather. Now that we were coming to the end of the trip, Ryan came round and asked us what we wanted to do. Unanimously, the show of hands said we were going to stay. On the brink of the summit we were hardly going to go home. With the summit in sight, we were not concerned about being there a few extra days or the added cost of missing scheduled flights. On summit day, we left early, taking the long rising traverse across snow to Denali Pass at 5,550 metres. From there, the route bore right up a very long but low-angled snow and ice slope between rock buttresses to Arch Deacon's Tower on the edge of the summit plateau. I was feeling strong, unlike I did on Anconcagua; Diamox tablets were helping me to acclimatise quicker. I should have used them on Aconcagua; a lesson learnt. From the plateau, a short descent led to 'The Football Field' and to the final climb along the short ridge to the summit of Denali.

On reaching the summit, I felt strong and I could have walked further. Unfortunately, my camera did not work but this did not take away my sense of achievement. Sledge pulling, digging caches and building walls out of snow should have sapped my strength but all I could feel was exhilaration. We could not jump around too much as it was a small summit with no markers. As the trip had overrun, we had to hightail down the mountain as fast as possible. We retraced our steps, stopping at each camp to pick up gear and rubbish, fearing the strict fines of the authorities. As the day wore on, I found the yellow bucket we used as a toilet, among the rubbish on my sledge. The sledge became a pain because it was relatively light and, therefore, it was difficult to keep under control. It kept banging the back of my legs and tipping over. I appropriately named the sledge 'The Pig'. It was trying my fragile, fatigued, dehydrated and hungry patience. The knots on my sledge worked loose until eventually the yellow toilet rolled down the hill out of reach. I stopped, slowly looked up at Ryan and said, 'I'll hang on, I do not need to go.' Eventually, the long grueling journey took us back to the Kahiltna Glacier. Everybody was queuing up, like waiting in line at passport control at the airport. The drama was not to end there as when the first plane came in, upon touching down, it flipped up so that its propeller became stuck in snow, leaving the body of the plane standing vertically like a column. Observing this, seated on our rucksacks, our jaws dropped. It was like something out of a Laurel and Hardy film. Everybody ran on to the runway to help right the plane. Thankfully, the plane flew off without anybody on it. I have never seen anything like that at Heathrow.

We did eventually all get back to Talkeetna where we had a lively night. Founded in 1916, Talkeetna is a colourful village with a long history of gold mining, which still continues today. It is a popular destination for outdoor enthusiasts, tourists and fishermen. In the next few days I said goodbye to my friends. I wished Rob and Jo well on their adventure, promising to follow it with interest. Jim was thrilled to have summited without frostbite. Jack, even with his old gear, had succeeded. He wished me well and said I was by far the strongest in our group apart from the leader. Jack's parting words to me were that one day I would go on to climb Everest. Ryan's parting words were, 'Denali is like a 7,000-metre peak in the Himalaya.'

CHAPTER 6

UNFINISHED BUSINESS

If at first you don't succeed then
come back and try again at a later date.

— ED BUCKINGHAM

Mountains will always be there but I am well aware I only have one life; it's important to know when to turn back, no matter how close the summit. If the moment is not right, sometimes you have to hold your hand up and say it was not meant to be. This was the case for me and Mont Blanc. It took me three attempts before I 'bagged it', as the saying goes. Having conquered both Aconcagua and Denali, which were far more demanding expeditions, I returned to the Alps because, relatively speaking, they were on my doorstep. The highest mountain in Europe (at 4,810 metres) outside the Caucasus region, Mont Blanc lies between France and Italy. Translated it means 'White Mountain'. In 1760, Horace-Bénédict de Saussure, a doctor from Geneva, offered a prize to the first person to climb Mont Blanc. In 1786, two local mountaineers, Michel Paccard and Jacques Balmat claimed the prize. Saussure himself climbed the mountain the following year.

According to Mont Blanc Guides, the ascent is not technically difficult and even inexperienced mountaineers can achieve it if they are fit and determined. Most climbers require at least three days to acclimatise to the altitude before attempting the ascent. Mont Blanc Guides offers a six-day course that includes training, acclimatisation walks and they supply equipment and accommodation in mountain huts.

I made two trips to the Alps in the summer of 2004. The first time I went for a week in Chamonix, our leader was an experienced guide from Scotland. I got the impression he was looking for some easier work outside life on the mountains. Though there must be a lot of enjoyment gained from the freedom of working outdoors, most of the guides know someone who has suffered tragedy. It must play at the back of their minds that the dice may fall on them one day. The rest of the group were of mixed ability. Clinton had little experience and found some of the days daunting. He was often seen leaning over on his haunches panting, out of breath. Catherine from Leeds and Victor from Russia were of similar ability to me. The three of us were reasonably fit and got on well with each other. During the week, we were able to get some acclimatisation walks in; we took the train up to Montenvers at 1,908 metres and walked on to the Mer de Glace.

We did have some bad weather. One particular afternoon, Catherine, Victor and I were on a rope with the guide. The wind had got up and was now gusting, making it very inhospitable indeed. At a time when we were looking for confidence from those around us, the guide just lost it shouting and raging at our incompetence. I was at the back of the rope and never felt as though we were losing control. Okay, the rope did meander a bit to start with but once Victor and Catherine dug in with strong feet and firm hands, we maintained a line. The guide was still chuntering on when we got further down and were more sheltered from the elements. Privately, I thought that if I were a novice, this sort display of emotion would not improve my confidence. Okay, there are times to act on impulse but not to lambast your clients openly. I had not witnessed this behaviour before. When we were in a white-out on Denali, Ryan calmly guided us to the wand marker of the next camp, by way of compass and sense of direction, with the help of Bill and Clark. Though he was under pressure, he performed well and gained our respect. Sure enough, the weather did become worse as the week progressed. Too bad to ascend Mont Blanc, we instead went up the 4,061-metre Gran Paradiso, a mountain in the Graian Alps just over the border in Italy. While the Mont Blanc massif straddles the border between France and Italy, the Gran Paradiso is the only mountain entirely within Italian territory whose summit reaches over 4,000 metres, so it could be considered the highest peak in Italy.

Mont Blanc took all the bad weather, while the mountains behind experienced milder conditions. It was all a bit the 'Lord Mayor's Show' for me. I had been thwarted yet again, but vowed to come back. Catherine and Victor felt the same way and together we travelled back to the Alps during a short weekend in August. The ratio of guides to clients is two to one so we hired two guides – Jean and Johnny. Private guiding is more expensive, especially in Chamonix at high season. It was to be third time lucky and without the constraints of a larger group, we moved a lot quicker. I was on the rope behind Jean, with Catherine bringing up the rear. We were experiencing a window of good weather and I was determined that this time, I would reach the summit. I needed no energy gels or drinks, my stimulation came from my frustration of having to come back a third time. My legs were working like pistons in a steam engine. I kept on Jean's heels all the way. Afterwards, Catherine said that she felt as though she was being dragged along by me. Jean said I had very strong legs and I had no problem keeping up. The small summit of Mont Blanc is a bit like Denali. It is an exposed ridge, which allows little margin for error, or else we would have plunged down like the white surf of a wave curling. This is why guides only guide two people maximum. If need be, guides can short-rope clients on the descent to give them greater control. I kept thinking back to my childhood in Cornwall when we used to walk along coastal paths as a family. My brother, Chris, used to walk too close to the edge and my mother would regularly tell him off. Following my previous achievements, Mont Blanc was not a problem for me. I came to the conclusion that a successful ascent was very weather dependent.

Fancying a winter getaway, I booked a holiday in Morocco in the Toubkal region. Although geographically very close to Europe, Morocco's human and physical geography is very different. The Atlas Mountains are the highest and most extensive range in North Africa, stretching around 2,500 kilometres through Morocco, Algeria and Tunisia. The Moroccan sub-range of the Atlas hosts the High Atlas region. This region generally comprises fairly gentle limestone formations but, in contrast the Jebel Toubkal area, is distinctive in its stark volcanic peaks. Rising out of the haze to the south of Marrakesh, the High Atlas offered us an incredible variety of scenery, a superb network of trails and challenging peaks. At 4,167 metres, Mount Toubkal is the highest peak in the Atlas and in North Africa.

In our group, there were eight English clients with hill-walking experience but they did not have much experience of winter walking. The guides were locals to the area. Both were named Muhammad. We were travelling during Ramadan, the ninth month of the Islamic calendar when Muslims worldwide observe a month of fasting. Ramadan means 'scorching heat' or 'dryness'. The annual observance is regarded as one of the five pillars of Islam. The month lasts twenty-nine to thirty days, based on the sightings of the crescent moon. Muslims fast from dawn until sunset, during which time they do not consume food, drink liquids or smoke. Food is served before sunrise and after sunset.

After a few days acclimatising on local peaks, we turned our attention to the highest mountain in the region. As we took our first steps to Toubkal, at 4,167 metres, I knew today was going to be difficult. I have never entertained missing a meal and I was feeling much worse for it. Lethargy and loud grumblings in my stomach are not pleasurable to me. I find that if I haven't eaten, I just end up gorging more food later on to make up what I've missed out on. Mountaineers need to replace the calories they burn in order to survive. Setting off from the Neltner Refuge, we made our way up the mountain, traversing the slope. I thought we should have had crampons on because many of us were slipping. I had rigid plastic winter mountaineering boots on which helped. Muhammad I was cutting steps with an ice-axe but he was finding it hard work, so, naturally, I helped. I ended up cutting more steps than him, as his energy levels dwindled. Not long afterwards he slipped, losing a glove and ice-axe down the mountain. He wasn't carrying a spare so he asked the other clients if he could borrow one of theirs. I advised them not to give up their ice-axes because it would compromise their movement. In winter mountaineering, everybody is advised to carry spare gloves and hats and not to provide for others. Peter, Dave and Ali began turning to me for guidance. They had lost confidence in Muhammad I after seeing him slip and knowing he was ill-prepared, having not brought spare gloves and wearing flexible walking boots unsuitable for the snow. We slowly made our way up, under the burning midday sun. Now I found myself ahead of the leader, Muhammad I, who was clearly knackered and happy for me to shoulder the burden of cutting steps. We did summit and rested there awhile, taking pictures, eating and drinking. Of course, the guides did not join us because of their religion.

On the descent, I was at the front, meandering down the steps made earlier. On one corner, Susan, a physiotherapist from Scotland, slipped and was now careering down the mountain at speed. As I heard her scream, I turned and saw her sliding like a bobsled. I shouted, 'Ice-axe arrest, ice-axe arrest. Dig the axe into the snow and get your body on top of it.' I repeated it, shouting loudly and clearly. Luckily Susan was a regular hill-walker in Scotland and knew what to do in an emergency.

Sure enough, under my instruction, she threw herself on to her axe and came to an abrupt halt. I was now the nearest one to her and went to assist. She was clearly shaken from the shock of what had happened. Of course, the first thing she saw was blood from a graze near her eye. I carefully cleaned it with an antiseptic wipe from my first-aid kit. Talking to her softly and calmly, I asked her if she had broken anything or if she was experiencing pain elsewhere. She said she had no broken bones, just a pain in her lower back.

By now the others had made their way down to us. I gave Susan ibuprofen and she said she felt she could walk as long as I stayed with her, which is exactly what I did. I walked slowly in front with my two poles, cutting steps to make it easier. I told Muhammad I to look after the rest while I took care of Susan. Once off the snow, Muhammad I wanted to put Susan on a mule, saying that progress was slow. Susan protested, saying that riding a mule was worse for her back and that she could walk on her own, as long as she was not under pressure to move quickly. I supported her, walking at her speed and giving her another dose of painkillers as we chatted. The next time I saw the group, Muhammad I and II were on the mule, clearly hungry, tired and exhausted from the ordeal of the day. In the coming weeks, I found out Susan had damaged her sacrum but she was profoundly grateful for what I did that day. The whole group wrote letters to the tour company explaining what had happened – a near fatality. I even took the trouble of ringing them to say the expedition should not operate during Ramadan. Needless to say, the holiday still featured in the following year's brochure. Common sense does not prevail when there is a chance to make a buck or two.

The following April, I was standing on Tower Bridge in London, watching the London Marathon. My brother was running in aid of Cancer Research. To my right was a tall figure that looked familiar. As our eyes met, he recognised me. It was Mike from my 1999 Kilimanjaro expedition. As we shook hands he heartily explained that Liz was running the marathon. Since Kilimanjaro, he had been diagnosed with cancer and, like my brother, Liz was running to raise some money for charity. Something that had been at the back of my mind was raising money for heart disease for people like my father. But Ryan's words had resonated with me, 'Denali is like a 7,000-metre peak in the Himalaya.'

The Himalaya is known for its historical, religious and geographical significance and, of course, its mountains. It served as a guard against various invasions, a border and a meeting ground for different races, culture and religion. It formed a divide between India and Tibet. But this barrier has not stopped individuals from pursuing adventurous journeys and exploring the unknown side of the mountains. People travelled for religious and trade purposes. The Himalayan region was a key centre for trade and commerce. With the famous Silk Route, this region first gained importance during the early Han dynasty 206 BC to AD 8. The route connected Central Asia with South Asia and created a bridge between culturally and religiously diverse countries such as India, China, Afghanistan, Nepal and Bhutan. The Himalaya was also a witness to the Indus Valley Civilisation, the oldest Indian Civilisation. In 1856, in the foothills of the Himalaya, the twin cities of Mohenjo-daro and Harappa were discovered giving it an historical background to unfold.

Now coming to the origin of the Himalaya, it can be said that millions of years ago a collision between the Indo Australian plate and the Eurasian plate resulted in the formation of the world's highest mountains. There were several steps in the formation of the Himalaya. The first step was the collision of the Gondwana plate and Angara plate. The seabed raised into longitudinal ridges and valleys. In the second step, the collision was very effective and powerful. The Tethys bed rose to a great extent to cause the final retreat of the sea. During this, the Great Himalaya and the Tibetan Himalaya were formed. In the third step the Lower Himalaya was formed. During the fourth step the Himalaya ranges elevated and the Sub Himalaya were raised. The last step was the final phase which determines the present structure of the Himalaya.

The panoramic view of the mountain ranges attracts travellers from across the world. The early Aryans considered the Himalaya to be the abode of Gods and Goddesses. In 1852, the highest mountain in the world, Mount Everest, was named after Sir George Everest. As Nepal opened its frontiers in 1949 to the outside world, people explored ten of the fourteen 8,000-metre peaks. Annapurna (8,091 metres) was the first peak to be climbed in 1950. Mount Everest (8,848 metres) and Nanga Parbat (8,125 metres) followed in 1953. From that time onwards, many expeditions have been made and by 1964 all the Himalayan 8,000-metre peaks had been climbed. Mount Everest was opened for mountaineering in the early 1920s but it was not until May 1953 that the first successful ascent was made by Tenzing Norgay and Edmund Hillary.

CHAPTER 7

THE HIMALAYA

*The great white sweep. A never-ending ocean of colossal
resplendent mountains, blinding in their brilliance
as they reach out to the cobalt blue sky.*

— ALAN HINKES

The Himalaya is home to the world's highest mountains, including the fourteen 8,000-metre peaks, nestled within five countries, Pakistan, India, China, Nepal and Bhutan. Many daunting challenges await those who seek adventure among the highest peaks, such as the sheer vertical scale, climatic conditions, avalanches, and frightful altitude sickness. Lack of oxygen to the brain and subsequent mountain sickness cause major problems such as acute pulmonary and cerebral oedema. Climbers must be prepared to take their lives in their hands and risk permanent damage to the body and brain as a result of anoxia. Driven by the possibility of bagging the biggest, they put their bodies through rigours and border on meltdown, coping with fatigue, cold, insomnia, diminished appetite and psychogenic stress.

All the 8,000-metre peaks take the climber into what is dubbed the 'Death Zone', an unforgiving environment in which the body starts to deteriorate to the point where it actually starts to die. It is not possible for a human being to survive for long beyond a couple of days above 8,000 metres. If you get a problem you are in a lot of trouble; there are no helicopters and no rescue teams. Simply surviving takes tremendous effort, both physically and mentally. All water needs to be melted from snow, breathing is difficult, food almost impossible to digest, sleep is unlikely and frostbite common.

The very low oxygen levels on the peaks have created debate as to whether or not a climber should use bottled oxygen. George Mallory himself described the use of oxygen as unsportsmanlike. In 1920, Mallory argued 'that the climber does best to rely on his natural abilities, which warn him whether he is overstepping the bounds of his strength. With artificial aids, he exposes himself to the possibility of sudden collapse if the apparatus fails.' However, on his final attempt at climbing Everest he did concede to using supplemental oxygen. Most, if not all commercial expeditions use oxygen. Everest has been climbed without the use of supplementary oxygen but only a few times by exceptionally fit and acclimatised mountaineers.

Since Denali, in 2003, I had replayed Ryan's last words to me, 'Denali is like a 7,000-metre peak in the Himalaya.' Having experienced almost 7,000-metres on Aconcagua, I now wanted to go a step further. Cho Oyu is the sixth highest mountain in the world at 8,201 metres. Even though it is regarded as technically straightforward, its altitude is a serious undertaking, requiring careful preparation and a high level of fitness. Cho Oyu means 'Goddess of Turquoise' as its stark shadows appear this colour in the light of the setting sun, when viewed from Tibet.

Cho Oyu has become a popular mountain. Its accessibility is a big draw. The ascent to the summit is short and direct with a few small technical sections, which are usually climbed using fixed ropes. Base Camp is reached by four-wheel drive vehicles. To reach Camp 1, at 6,400 metres, it is a steady but steep walk usually done in trekking boots rather than mountaineering boots. Like all high mountains the weather is extremely changeable. At lower elevations the temperatures can be blisteringly hot at midday and well below freezing once the sun sets. A climber can experience everything from a flat calm to hurricane force winds on the summit.

Categorising any 8,000-metre peak as 'easy' or referring to an 'ordinary' or 'normal' route to the summit is a contradiction in terms. There is nothing easy or normal about any 8,000-metre mountain. These mountains are serious undertakings, with many dangers. However, Cho Oyu is generally regarded as the easiest and safest of the fourteen. Avalanches and rockfall are less likely on Cho Oyu as there are fewer steep slopes.

My trip to the Himalaya was relatively short, around five weeks altogether, but the longest for me so far. Without taking unpaid leave, I used most of my year's allocation of annual leave for one trip. Apart from the days when I was assigned a 4 a.m. start at work, I trained hard. Once I was committed to this trip, my drive, determination and motivation were there. Again, I could not afford to go to the Alps to prepare so I made use of my surroundings in Cornwall. I undertook cardiovascular training four times a week, including running, swimming and walking. Once a week, I walked for five to eight hours carrying a pack, weighing twenty-five kilograms, in mountaineering boots. The weight was cumbersome and heavy but it helped to strengthen my mind. Since Denali, I was starting to see a change in me. I was losing my puppy fat and my muffin top. Overweight mountaineers are a rarity indeed.

I met the group in Kathmandu, Nepal. It was a big group of nineteen international members, including five Brits. Tunc Findik from Turkey had already climbed Everest and Lhotse (8,516 metres), and he was by far the fittest and would be the first up Cho Oyu. Doug Cote, Thierry Auberson, Guntis Brands, Herve Coron and Johan Frankelius all had experience in the US and Europe. Austrian Gernot Gessinger was the oldest and had the advantage of living at altitude in the Alps. Of the five Brits, I had the most mountaineering experience but Dominic Faulkner did have an army background. The two expedition leaders were Arnold Coster and Phil Crampton. Arnold originated from Holland but was now living in Nepal. His local knowledge and contacts were extensive in the Himalayan region. His relaxed, easy approach helped when trying to climb an 8,000-metre peak. The other leader, Phil, originated from Nottingham and lived in New York. My first impression was that he reminded me of the actor Hugh Grant and he would not have looked out of place in Hollywood. The Tibetan cooks on the expedition were trained in Phil's restaurant in New York. We also had Maya Sherpa with us, the first Nepalese woman to climb Cho Oyu.

Following a final kit inspection, we made last minute purchases of any missing equipment in the many stores in Kathmandu square. We scrutinised the equipment carefully to check it was up to the task. Leaving Kathmandu, we caught the bus to Kodari, the last town in Nepal. From there we crossed the Friendship Bridge over the Bota Kosi River. We travelled up the Friendship Highway north through Nepal to Tibet. Thankfully, the road was free of landslides and we drove to the Zhangmu border. It was quite amusing as we hauled our luggage across the bridge; we were like refugees escaping. We had to clear Nepalese customs and immigration to get into Tibet. Like in Moscow, I tried to take photographs but finger pointing and stern looks stopped me rather abruptly. The gateway town in Tibet is Zhangmu where we stayed for the night. Over the next two days, we travelled by Land Cruiser to the towns of Nyalam and Tingri, at 4,300 metres. I was not impressed with Tibetan food. Noodles and rice swimming in water are not particularly tasty and I was fearful the food contained bacteria. I was concerned about becoming ill, of which some of the group were already complaining. I found myself buying crisps, biscuits and chocolate, which was not ideal but it was crucial to stay strong and healthy as we weren't even on the mountain yet. I saw a flea-ridden dog chewing a carcass on a spit in the middle of the street, which certainly didn't encourage me to eat.

Thankfully, the following morning, we made the forty-four-kilometre journey to Cho Oyu Base Camp, at 4,900 metres. What a relief it was to be on camp food. I had escaped catching anything by not eating the food served in Zhangmu, Nylam and Tingri. Tingri is a dirty, bare, dusty, inhospitable mud-walled village. I envisaged Clint Eastwood, in the film *High Plains Drifter*, covered in brown and grey dust and yak dung. It's usually a good idea to stop for a few days in Nyalam, 1,000 metres lower down, in order to acclimatise gradually and safely. Since our arrival in Nepal, we had been travelling by vehicle. No amount of training can prepare a climber for altitude of this magnitude. I was nervous and concerned. In the next couple of days we proceeded to Advanced Base Camp, at 5,600 metres, via an intermediate camp at 5,300 metres. We needed to take enough equipment for one night's stop so we divided up our kit for the yaks to carry. Yaks are a distinctly familiar sight around the Himalaya. It is not uncommon to see yak trains, with their distinctive bells, coupled together, almost skewering the one in front. It's a pity more cyclists back home do not use bells when they approach from behind and want to pass. Quiet and docile, they are used to carrying huge weights up to Advanced Base Camp. It was funny to watch the herders bartering over loads with the expedition leaders. They often thought the bulkier items, such as the blue barrels that kept our equipment safe and dry, weighed the most, when often this was not the case. A set of scales often settled any disputes.

We had a funny experience at the intermediate camp. While we lay in our tents we could hear water running nearby. Melting snow had begun to trickle down the mountain. It wasn't quite the Boscastle floods of 2004 but we had to quickly evacuate and move our tents. Between Base and Advanced Base, Dominic developed a chest infection. This didn't bode well as we were still at a relatively low altitude. Once diagnosed by a doctor, he made the decision to stop and go back. He tried descending for a few days in the hope that he was able to make a recovery and come back but, unfortunately, the chest infection was too serious. Such a shame when you consider the time, effort and money it takes to go on these expeditions. We set up at Advanced Base Camp. We had the privacy of an individual tent and shared the mess tent.

Over the next couple of days, we started to carry up to Camp 1, at 6,400 metres. Just as on Aconcagua, we were split into groups, each travelling separately. Tunc, Thierry, Guntis, Herve and Johan all went up before me with their first carries. My first journey up to Camp 1 was a hard slog, taking between four and six hours up the Gyabrag Glacier, along steep scree to a broad snow shoulder. By the time I returned, I was tired. After my experience on Aconcagua, I disciplined myself to drink during the night and early in the morning. Sleeping is an exercise and the body does dehydrate. I benefited from feeling hydrated, starting the day without a headache. Some members of the team had been quarantined in their own tents at mealtimes to stop infection spreading, which was very concerning. I made a conscious effort to cough into my arm rather than my hand and not share personal hand gels. Following a night at Camp 1, we explored some of the route to Camp 2, which lies at 7,100 metres. This was the most challenging part of the climb. We made the ascent, following the ridge out of Camp 1 to a steep fifty-metre ice wall on fixed rope. I made it to about 6,700 metres to the base of the ice wall before going back down to Advanced Base Camp. The next time I went up, there had been heavy snowfall the night before so I had to break trail – this makes the ascent more difficult but I had experienced this on Denali. Walking to Camp 2 was a hard day for me, negotiating a 700-metre ascent and the ice wall. On reaching Camp 2, I was knackered; 7,100 metres was new territory for me.

My powers of recovery seemed to be on top form because after a good night's rest, I went back down feeling fine. That was the end of the acclimatisation programme. Next time I went up, I would be going to Camp 3, at 7,500 metres, and then onward to the summit. Worryingly, the illness going around camp had begun to affect the guides as well as the clients. Tunc had already summited, proving he was by far the fittest. Summiting two 8,000-metre peaks prior to our expedition had helped. Thierry and François from Switzerland had both failed in their first attempt to summit but with so much time left, they could try again when their bodies had recovered. It is widely believed that your best attempt is your first, as the body gives the most into it. Recovery for another attempt in one season is rare and fortunate. I was not fazed: if I had only one real go at this, I was going to give it my best shot.

Making it back to Camp 2, my next target was Camp 3 at 7,500 metres. The ground was easier to walk on but after a tough previous day, traversing higher was hard. To get to Camp 3, we slowly went up a very steep slope, taking our time. It reminded me of Motorcycle Hill on Denali, but steeper. Seeing the stove suspended in the entrance of the tent was a very welcome sight indeed, like a house on a hill. I had done well but I was in for some bad news: a guide had gone down ill, meaning I would have to double up with Ben on my summit push. Privately, I was not happy. Ben had been a lot quicker than me during the trip and I felt I would be now pressurised to go at his speed.

Some people were using oxygen higher up, which was a personal choice not a policy. Above 7,800 metres, in the 'Death Zone', even with the use of supplementary oxygen, the body is not designed to be there. Ben and I both chose not to use oxygen but I had strong reservations about the forthcoming night. At 2 a.m. we made our way uphill on fixed lines through a rock band, with the aid of our head torches. Once we had come through the other side, I found myself lagging behind the other two members of my groups. My fear of not being able to keep up with Ben was soon realised. If I carried on at this speed, I would burn out so I made the decision to join another group and settled into a more comfortable pace. Thankfully the weather was good and I still felt confident about summiting. Further on, the route went over moderate snow and rock. My new team members were slowing down and I now felt they were cramping me a bit. In the light, I had full vision of what was going on around me and I found myself walking on my own. For what seemed like hours, I plodded through the greyish-white opaque world, slowly gaining height. I was concentrating on finding the highest point. The expansive, featureless, snow-covered summit of Cho Oyu is reminiscent of a Cairngorm hilltop, only bigger. It might as well have been an expanded Ben Macdui plateau, transported from Scotland, in winter, to Tibet, but without an Ordnance Survey trig pillar to mark the highest point.

Before I reached the summit, I saw my guide and Ben returning. The guide wished me good luck and uttered, 'Not far to go now.' I felt he should have stayed with me, walking with the slowest man. I made it to the broad expanse of the summit. It reminded me of a big field back home in Cornwall, but with Makalu in the background. Turning to my left, I had to look up. Towering before my eyes was Everest in all its glory. It had taken all my reserves to get to 8,200 metres. Everest is a further 648 metres but it looked like a challenge akin to scaling the Eiffel Tower. I felt extremely privileged and honoured to have got this far. Like on all summits, there is a limited time to enjoy the view before the descent. Apart from on Kilimanjaro, I have always gone down the same route I came up. My body, mind and my mountain instinct were telling me that I needed to get to a lower altitude. My focus was now on finding the route back and I made my return journey through the rocky band back to high camp. Thankfully some bamboo wands, like golf course flags, had been left to mark the route.

Once within the rocky bands of bare rock, I took more care not to trip or fall, crampons are not designed for bare rock but it is tiring and energy-consuming to keep taking them on and off. I could see Camp 3 ahead of me while I was on top of the steepest part of the climb near the summit. I remembered it from going up in the dark. I am not sure what put me off but I think a combination of high altitude, fatigue, lack of concentration, no poles and no guide made me hesitate. I went off the path to my right where I thought it was easier to descend. In doing so, I tripped over bare rock and went glissading down the mountain. I was experiencing the same thing Susan had on Toubkal, except this was steeper, creating a greater velocity. I was taught to always hold my ice-axe near my head to self-arrest. This is what I had to do, and fast, taking a couple of goes to slow myself, like a car braking in wet conditions. Finally I stopped; I had slid around 150 metres. I drew breath and took in my surroundings. I was now below Camp 3, meaning I had to climb back but, in the fall, I had lost a crampon. Phil Crampton was at Camp 3 and had seen me sliding. The team at Camp 3 could not help me as they had no ropes and, unbeknown to me, I was in crevasse territory. Phil and Andy Sloan, the next climber to attempt the summit that night, could only shout to me and offer encouragement as I staggered back up the mountain, minus a crampon. Fatigue, dehydration and hunger were all affecting me now. Having already climbed further than I ever had before, I had to dig deep into my energy reserves and find the willpower to continue or else I would perish and become just another statistic. I kept thinking, 'no mountain is worth a life, coming back is a success and summiting is only a bonus'.

It took me about an hour to get up to them; I was absolutely cream-crackered and breathless. Phil stood there guard-like, gobsmacked. I looked up at him smiling and said, 'Have you got the kettle on? I could do with a brew.' At the time, I was using plastic boots with an inner sole. I took off the outer shell and climbed in my sleeping bag with my sweaty socks and inners on. Nick Williams and Matt Ward had succumbed to the mountain, leaving Andy Sloan, the remaining Brit. I wanted to help him by boiling water for food and drink. He had made the decision to use oxygen but was sick after having noodles. Of course, each time a climber is sick it causes further dehydration and high altitude only exacerbates the problem. I wished him well for his summit attempt, before retiring to my tent. I can remember him and Phil setting off, rustling like mice in their tents. A couple of days later, they told me I had been snoring loudly – another product of high altitude.

The next day a Tibetan helper came up from Advanced Base Camp with crampons, courtesy of Arnold. Arnold was fully aware of what had happened to me as he was in contact with Phil via radio and had been watching my precarious predicament through binoculars. On the descent, my toes felt particularly sore and painful. Plastic boots are not that comfortable and I put it down to the fact that my toes were constantly being pushed against the front of the boot. Approaching Camp 1, I noticed crevasses near to the tents, which had not been there when we had first pitched. The climbing season was nearing its end, like the summer holidays finishing at the end of August in Cornwall. It was time to get off the mountain. Clearing the tent, I went down the scree slope to Advanced Base Camp. I got a huge cheer and slaps on the back for my effort and endurance. Arnold's dispatch the day before had only gone out as saying, 'Edward had a long and epic day'. Dispatches were posted on the internet daily so relatives and family could follow our progress at home. I had been concerned that my family had learnt of my fall before I got down the mountain. If it can be avoided, I prefer to keep away from any histrionics.

Out of nineteen members, only ten had summited, proving how tough and unforgiving the mountain is. The cooks made cake to celebrate. It was amazing what they could do at that height, using ingredients so different from those I cook with at home. Once in my tent, I peeled my inner boots and socks off my tender feet. Staring at me were two big toes and four little toes covered in blisters and frostbite, reminding me of Jim's photos from Denali. This was a result of my negligence in not taking my socks off and drying my feet the night before – a schoolboy error. I immediately went to Arnold for inspection and advice. He told me to keep my feet elevated as much as possible for the next three days and, more importantly, to not burst the blisters and risk infection. That is what I did while the team cleared the mountain of rubbish and equipment. Over the next few days, I saw the other side of mountaineering. The summiteers were arguing vehemently about who had summited first and within what time. I realised how competitive this sport is and it could even explain why so many lives are lost on the mountains. I was just thankful I was alive and relatively unharmed. When I did come to walk again, I was lucky the swelling had gone down sufficiently to put my trekking boots on. But I was concerned about what long-term damage I had done to my feet and the impact it would have on my career with Royal Mail.

On returning to Kathmandu, Arnold took me to the Travel Medicine Centre. Doctors Eyal Lesham and David Kraklau iodine-bathed my feet and dressed them with bulky bandages. They also started me on a course of ibuprofen and cephalexin. It was still unclear what damage I had done. During our remaining days in Kathmandu, I went back to the doctors daily to have my feet soaked and to have the dressings replaced. I was advised to go immediately to my family doctor once I got home. With my oversized bandages and sandals on, I was quite a sight for my parents when I stepped out of Plymouth station, towards the end of October. I must have looked like Bugs Bunny walking along the platform. I was gaunt and haggard from the exertion of my venture. The first words I said to my parents were, 'If you ever see me on another bloody mountain again, shoot me'. This was in reference to the words spoken by Sir Steve Redgrave as he got out of his rowing boat having just won his fourth Olympic gold medal. But the strong antibiotics killed the infection, and my swollen blisters went down. These were positive signs that I had not done any long-term damage. That evening, I stayed at my parents' house. Laying down in the living room, I fell asleep like a dog after a long hard walk, content by the fire.

Down at my family GP, I was the talk of the surgery. All the doctors and nurses came and had a look. This was a real experience for them, having only previously seen frostbite in books and on the internet. Thankfully the journey had not traumatised my feet any more. In fact, I would not lose any toes, I had just bruised my tendons a bit, meaning my feet could be more susceptible to the cold. But after painting the toes with iodine, in time, I lost the skin and toenails on the blackened areas. It was a small price to pay. I felt a right girl painting my toes and wearing extra socks that coming winter, but the positives far outweighed the negatives. I did not lose any toes and I was able to go back to my regular routine of working in distribution for Royal Mail. My desire to be an outdoor worker was not taken away from me. I had come back from a near tragedy and had shown tremendous courage, spirit and resilience in overcoming adversity. To climb the sixth highest mountain in the world without oxygen is no mean feat.

CHAPTER 8

MAKING A COMEBACK FROM SETBACKS

All thoughts of future mountaineering are firmly
put on the back burner. The fight now is
to return to full and active duty.

— ED BUCKINGHAM

Turning to change direction on AstroTurf, I felt my left knee crack, like walnuts crunching in a nutcracker. I hobbled through the pain for the rest of the game and went to bed that night thinking it was only a knock and that it would be back to normal after a few days; not this time. The next day, boy had the knee swollen up. By 7 a.m. I was in accident and emergency at Derriford in Plymouth. The swelling was so bad I was told to rest up and keep an ice pack on it so the bruising came out. The swelling had to go down before an X-ray was taken to ascertain the extent of the damage. The following week, I was diagnosed with damaged knee ligaments. I braced my knee for work and struggled on manfully with the help of ice packs and resting when I could. My movements became alien to normal, over-compensating for my injury. After about four weeks, I had had enough. My lower back was feeling sore – I had begun to experience problems that could stay with me into later life.

At the back of my mind, I had a bigger problem. I could not carry on like this, I needed to be told the truth and get my knee put right. I had just moved into my third property with bigger doors and a downstairs toilet, where incapacitated people could live without the need to go upstairs. I did not foresee that, at the age of thirty-four, I would be moving into a property with this in mind.

In my first consultation with Patrick Loxdale, an orthopaedic surgeon, he assessed me and announced that I need not have an operation. He said, 'To look at Edward, he does not have the physiology of an athlete and when he touched on mountaineering I understood it as being Snowdon. But when he went on to explain he climbed Cho Oyu without oxygen, I conceded that he must have a pretty unique physiology.' He soon back-tracked when he saw my expression of alarm at the thought of trying to carry on with my present situation. I enjoyed working outdoors and had no plans on being restricted to indoor work. I told him that I had been struggling for around six weeks and that I wanted to get to the root of the problem and face any long-term consequences. Following an MRI scan, it was conclusive that I had ruptured the anterior cruciate ligament in my left knee. I was going to have an operation, meaning nine months without playing football and probably twelve before I could go back to mountain-eering. I would have to show a mental toughness of a different kind now. Never mind climbing the sixth highest mountain in the world, I had a battle to get back to a normal way of life. That was unforeseeable at the moment. What quality of life would I have after the operation? But, despite my concerns, I was keen to give the operation a go. It had to be worth a chance to see if my current situation could be improved upon. Pre-oper-ation, I managed to keep myself reasonably fit by swimming regularly. This was my priority, all thoughts of mountaineering were put on hold. I understood that I may never go mountaineering again.

Following the operation, I was faced with the long road to recovery. I was under strict medical orders not to do too much too soon and give my knee chance to heal. I corresponded regularly with my physio, Bev Derrick, at St Barnabus, in Saltash, and Patrick. Patrick stressed in this case not to push too hard in the physio, fearing that it would undo all the hard work of the operation. I didn't rush back to work but when I did return, I built my hours up slowly, starting on four hours a day and building up to a full shift over the course of a few weeks. Working at a mail centre, I was able to work indoors and undertake indoor sorting. I did not want the stress of normal operations and working in distribution but I was showing my employer that I was making a concerted effort in returning to work. It is quite ironic to think the indoors was, for the moment, my lifeline when I had always considered it my confinement.

Just under a year later, I had made rapid progress. I did not need to wear a brace, use ice packs or take ibuprofen and I had returned to normal operational work in distribution. Patrick told me that I may suffer tightness in my left hamstring from time to time where he had reconstructed the knee. Overall though, the operation had been a success and I had my quality of life back again. He also said that he saw no reason why I could not go back to mountaineering but he told me not to rush into a heavy challenge. This was the tonic I needed. My decision to have the operation and go through rehab had been a good one. I was able to walk, work and exercise unassisted. I didn't need a stick and I didn't walk with a limp. It was time to start planning for the future again.

I had already decided my football career would come to an end, as this was the second injury I had suffered. In the challenging times of modern industry and the continuing threat of privatisation, would a private company have been so supportive during my rehabilitation?

Throughout my recovery, by the power of the internet, I had been following Rob and Jo Gambi's progress. Since Denali, they had gone on to complete the seven summits, among a whole host of other ventures.

Clearly they had a very different budget to me. Most remarkably, they had climbed Everest. Recalling my trip to Denali, I was by far the strongest and fittest. What were my chances of climbing Everest? The idea was now in my head but first I had to see how robust my knee was.

I returned to mountaineering in 2008. I was in Bolivia and the Cordillera Real region just east of Lago Titicaca. Landlocked and isolated, Bolivia has a varied landscape, stretching from the icy peaks and dry high-altitude deserts of the Andes to the richly diverse rainforests and vast savannahs of the Amazon basin, The country also has a strong ethnic and cultural mix. The majority of Bolivians are of indigenous descent, and the strength of Amerindian culture here is perhaps greater than anywhere else in Latin America.

The whole country is dwarfed by the mighty Andes that runs west through the country in two parallel chains dotted with many 6,000-metre snow-capped peaks. Between the two chains of mountains stretches the Altiplano, a barren, treeless plateau that has historically been home to most of Bolivia's population and whose windswept expanses are perhaps the best known image of the country. North-east of the Altiplano, the Andes plunge abruptly down into the tropical rainforests and savannahs of the Amazon lowlands, a seemingly endless wilderness crossed by a series of major rivers that flow north to the Brazilian border and beyond. East of the Altiplano the Andes slope down more gradually through a drier region of fertile highland valleys that give way eventually to the eastern lowlands.

My trip and acclimatisation period began in La Paz. It has a spectacular setting, sitting 3,500 metres above sea level in a narrow canyon gorged from the high Altiplano. During the coming week we climbed some magnificent and shapely peaks, culminating in an attempt on Illimani, at 6,462 metres. Bolivia is known for having stable and reliable weather, giving me the ideal opportunity to test my rebuilt knee. A far cry from Denali and Cho Oyu, each day involved a rigorous walk in the mountains. We were a small group of around eleven members who, aside from me, had very little mountain experience. As all the members of the group were from Britain, the camaraderie between us struck up very early. Cecelio was one of two local guides and Supermario was our cook. He was to prove very popular with his mates while on the trek. During the trip we had a lot of sunshine and enjoyed several hours of walking in lighter clothing and sunhats. The region had a South American feel to it and the early days of trekking reminded me of the Horcones Valley in Argentina.

As the days past, we climbed Pyramid Austria, Bianca and Alpamayo. We were coming to the crucial days and our attempt on Illimani, at 6,462 metres, was imminent. Camping by a stagnant stream, I noticed the helpers taking water. When using stagnant water, it must be boiled longer than normal to kill any living bacteria. Back home, I always take water from a running stream or I use a filter. That night I went to bed feeling reasonably okay but in the early hours I was up, rushing to the toilet with diarrhoea. I had never been this bad during any of my previous trips. By the time the rest were up, I was feeling very dehydrated and tired. I made the decision not to go any further because I did not want to exacerbate the problem. The best way of recuperating was to descend to a lower level, where the air was thicker with oxygen and the food was not just an aid to survival but had more nutritional value. I wished Cecelio and the others well and remained in camp with Supermario. During that time, I joined him in the cook's tent, which was full of tins of quality food and soups. During the trip so far, I felt that the food served had been poor compared with the food on previous expeditions. I now saw why. Out of Cecelio's sight, Supermario was giving all his mates the good food and reheating the leftovers for us clients. Whether Cecelio knew or was just turning a blind eye to it, it certainly was not right. What a raw deal we were getting. No wonder I was feeling sick, lethargic and malnourished. It was small wonder more members of the team had not fallen ill before now. On returning from a successful summit, the others were bubbling, but they graciously recognised that if I had been well, I would have had no problems. I was feeling a lot better, in fact, not long after they had left, I had started to recover. Obviously I was frustrated but making sure my knee was okay was more important. I had had no recurring knee problems, aches, pains or cramps. Admittedly, it had not been the most arduous of trips and the level of difficulty was low. It gave me the confidence to attempt something much harder. Frustrated at the end of the trip, I hired a guide called Rudolpho and we climbed Huayna Potosí, at 6,088 metres. Like Mont Blanc, it was a twenty-four-hour foray to bag the summit. I reached the top and was pleased with the progress I had made. The altitude had proved no problem for me and, more importantly, my knee had stood up to the rigours of mountaineering.

My next trip took me back to where it all started – Kilimanjaro. I supported a friend and together we attempted the same route as I had ten years previously – the Machame. The first two days saw torrential rain in the rainforests soaking most members and their kit. By now, I had learnt to put all spare clothes and my sleeping bag in dry bags to ensure I had something dry to change into. Stopping for the first night in the rainforest, I was asked to go to a tent occupied by four women. Peering in, they asked me what to do as everything was soaking wet. I said that they should all sleep together to remain warm and to put any wet kit in the second tent. I privately prayed that we would have some dry weather.

Something caught my eye. Pegged next to some clothes on a washing line were the passport photos of a man who had been lost fighting in Afghanistan. These four ladies, including his wife, were walking in memory of him, to raise money for Help for Heroes. They came from Royal Wootton Bassett in Wiltshire where every time the Hercules flies in returning from conflicts, a fallen hero is brought home to be laid to rest. I decided I would help them in any way I could during the remainder of the trip. Though we had all set ourselves the same target of reaching the summit, there was much more significance behind these ladies' journey. We all made it to the summit, which did not surprise me, but the others were joyous. It did make me feel proud to have helped the four ladies in some way.

I found that the mountain was not as cold as it had been ten years ago, there was hardly any snow and the field of ice around the crater rim had almost melted. Summit night, the scree slope was not frozen and we could use a water Platypus without the tube freezing up. The guides explained this was the result of global warming and in ten to fifteen years there would be no snow at all. This begged the question, what will happen if, as predicted, the planet continues to warm up?

When I explained what I had achieved, the guides turned round and said, 'When are you going to climb Everest?' The truth is, this trip was easy for me. The fitness and stamina I had attained over the years, together with the knowledge I had gained during my trips, was still there. Even though I did not live at altitude, my body coped admirably with the demands and stress. I was now going home with this ringing in my ears. It is true that when I was looking through the brochures I was thinking it's pointless attempting a mountain less than Cho Oyu, so that left five others.

That winter, in 2009/2010, I went back on the words I had spoken in 2005. I now wanted to climb Everest, or at least give it my best shot. This would be my third time visiting the Himalaya. The first time, in 2000, I took a Buddha Air flight along some of the peaks. Like a slideshow waiting for the picture of Everest to come into view, I had my camera ready to get the all-important shot.

Once I had decided I was going, the first person I spoke to was my family GP, Dr Webster Harrison. He said I was fit enough to attempt it as long as I was aware of the risks I was taking. So then it was time to tell my family – firstly my brother and then my parents. I told them over a meal at my house, plying them with drink before dropping the line about wanting to climb Everest. They took it well really and I recall mother saying she always thought I would do it one day. They would worry about me, of course, but they gave me their blessing. Thinking back, it could not have been easy for them after seeing me returning from Cho Oyu in 2005. Now my aspiration was to climb 648 metres higher, but besides that, I wanted to raise money for the British Heart Foundation and become the first Cornishman to conquer Everest.

CHAPTER 9

THE JEWEL IN THE CROWN

Described as the 'smoking gun'. Plumes of wind sweeping across the summit by mid-morning seen from afar.

— ALAN HINKES

The Nepalese call it Sagarmatha, while the Tibetans, in the north, call it Chomolungma, 'Goddess Mother of the Earth'. Surveyors discovered the mountain in 1852 when it was given the name Everest, after the former British surveyor general of India, George Everest. Rising dramatically from the north and west, Everest's massive pyramid towers above Cho Oyu, Lhotse and Makalu. K2, in Pakistan is 250 metres lower, but technically more difficult. Everest is the apex of the Himalaya, which means 'abode of snow', the greatest mountain range in the world. It is the source of great rivers, sustaining the large population of the Indo-Gangetic plain. Anyone seeing those glittering summits for the first time cannot help but feel a little awed.

It is only latterly that the Sherpas, who live beneath Everest, have set foot on the slopes. For them, it is a high-risk job, not a hobby. Sherpas are considered to be highly privileged to have been brought up in Everest's huge shadow. Without their help and considerable knowledge very few foreigners hoping to summit would make it. Even the easier routes on Everest present more complex problems than any of the other seven summits. It is the effects of altitude, rather than the fact that it stands more than 2,000 metres higher than Aconcagua, that makes it a challenge for any climber. Any climber that reaches the summit stretches the limits of what the body can cope with. Few do it without supplementary oxygen but even with oxygen the chances of reaching the top are slight. The Sherpa staff prepare the route – fixing the lines and stocking higher camps. Anyone attempting this mountain should do so with caution.

For those seeking the ultimate masochistic challenge, it is possible to climb Everest in winter. Summit temperatures plummet to below minus forty degrees. Winds over 120 kilometres per hour blast away at the snow, leaving bare rock and iron-hard ice. The majority of ascents are made in the spring, teams usually arrive at Base Camp in early April with a view to summiting in mid-May. During this period, before the arrival of the monsoon, temperatures are comparatively warm and winds are not as vicious as they are in the autumn. Nevertheless, the weather is variable and can be very unsettled, especially in the afternoon when snow squalls are not uncommon. Success depends upon having a fine spell over four or five days, once a team has acclimatised.

In 1980, Reinhold Messner climbed the north face during the summer monsoon, which was traditionally considered too dangerous for climbing as it was the warmest, wettest time of year, with many avalanches on the mountain. Since this feat, few have repeated Messner's monsoon success. Post-monsoon attempts are usually a race against the coming winter winds, which hardly affect the lower peaks but are devastating above 7,000 metres. Frostbite is a much greater risk than in the spring and consequently success rates are much lower.

The South Col/South-East Ridge route is often derogatorily referred to as the 'yak route'. It is the most popular route up Everest but should never be underestimated. There are four main sections: the extremely dangerous Khumbu Icefall, the steady plod up the Western Cwm, the steeper 1,500-

metre-high Lhotse Face and the long summit ridge from the South Col. The North Ridge/North-East Ridge starts proper from Advanced Base Camp at 6,400 metres on the East Rongbuk Glacier. This line is shorter than the normal South Col route. Above the North Col, the route becomes increasingly rocky with some awkward terrain. Although the top camp is higher than the South Col route, the actual terrain on summit day is definitely harder. The legendary Second Step feels very precarious even with the ladder placed by the Chinese. On the final section, there are some delicate areas poised over an awesome drop down the North Face.

As soon as I had made the decision to climb Everest, I began to put a plan in motion. To climb Everest would cost well into five figures. Buying equipment I would not cut any corners and spend whatever was necessary to aid my well being. I needed twelve weeks' annual leave, meaning a two-year allocation entitlement and, on top of that, a further week unpaid. Either side of the trip I took no leave so I hoped everything would go according to plan. As soon as I said I was climbing Everest, the insurance cost went up dramatically, like buying a BMW as opposed to a Skoda. I bought new equipment – I was not cutting corners on Everest, not that I had up until now. Starting with the feet, I bought 8,000-metre boots with a built-in gaiter which alone cost me 800 pounds. I had inner socks made, which were designed to both wick any moisture and keep my feet warm. Since I developed frostbite on Cho Oyu, the damaged tissue had recovered with no long-term effects and I had good circulation. Nevertheless, I was taking no chances, at 7,620 metres, I could not just take my boots off to put on extra socks if my feet were cold. By the same token, sweating causes the core to cool quicker, leading to hypothermia. I spent one hundred pounds on a pair of mittens with a thumb and index finger. Mittens are warmer than gloves but I still needed to be able to use my hands. Working with gloves on the ascender and karabiners is an art and

1   Me, at almost one year old.
2   Contrary to popular belief, I always kept a close eye on my brother Chris.
3   Starting work for the Royal Mail in 1989 as a postal cadet on the Youth Training Scheme.
4   My final class photo at primary school, 1984. I am in the second row from the back, fifth from left. Scott Ivins is second from left, and Phil Pollard second from the right, seated. We now run together in the Tamar Trotters.

5   My first experience of waking up to the frost on Kilimanjaro, 1999.
6   Helicopter repatriation that you pay insurance for and hope you never use.
7   The dry, dusty, desolate heat of the Horcones Valley, Aconcagua 2001.
8   Elbrus was emotionally hard for me. July 2002.

9

10

9　Snowed in on Denali.
10　The feeling of isolation as the plane leaves Kahiltna Base Camp, Denali 2003.
11　Queuing on Mont Blanc.
12　Frostbite on Cho Oyu in 2005, although it could have been a lot worse!

11

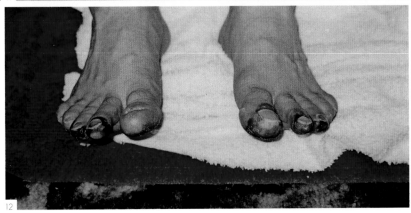

12

13

14

13 Looking up from the Rongbuk monastery through the prayer flags towards Everest. You can see the plumes of snow coming off the summit like a smoking gun.

14 Tenji Sherpa. Without these people we would not climb Everest. They are seriously undervalued by their governments.

15 The first Cornishman to summit Everest. I'm proudly holding the St Piran's flag, and I have Mia's giraffe.

16 & 17 The route up from Camp 3 to the ridge, negotiating the infamous Second Step before getting on to the triangular pyramid to the summit.

18 Kosciuszko, 2013. Can this really be considered one of the seven summits?

19 The sheer vastness of Antarctica. That it is still relatively unspoilt by man makes it a truly magical experience.

15

16

17

18

20

21

20 It did remind me of the New Zealand Pass. Though the emerald lakes are not shimmering on this occasion.

21 The Tyrolean traverse before reaching the summit on Carstensz. November 2014.

22 Upon returning home I spent some time on the British Heart Foundation stand at the Royal Cornwall Show, showing off my proud achievement.

23 Spending time with my nephew, Theo, and nieces, Mia and Jessica – there is never a dull moment. Sennen, October 2015.

24 With my parents, having been presented with the award for Exceptional Endeavour by the Cornish Gorsedh. September 2013.

25 Spending time with Fi. I see similar character traits in her as in myself. Liverpool marathon, June 2015.

26 The Matterhorn (4,478 metres), August 2015.

has to be practised. My brother used to say I had meat-cleaver hands, like shovels, from farming, but, over the course of time, my fingers had become thinner. After seeking advice, I made the decision to use oxygen. I bought five bottles before the trip so that I would not be panicking if I needed it in Nepal when demand and cost would be high.

Everest is a three-sided pyramid with the South-West Face in Nepal and the East and North Faces in Tibet. From the south, the mountain is obscured by Nuptse and Lhotse. Hidden behind this wall is an enclosed valley called the Western Cwm. This is the approach to the South-West Face and the high saddle called the South Col, from where the normal route continues up the South-East Ridge. The Western Cwm's glacier is squeezed out through a steep narrow corridor, tumbling in a chaos of jumbled rocks known as the Khumbu Icefall, an unavoidable danger on the southern routes. For this reason, many Sherpas prefer the route up from Tibet and the North-East Ridge.

The East Face is the biggest and most dangerous of Everest. Like many faces in the Himalaya, it is draped with spectacular snow flutings and hanging glaciers, poised above formidably steep rock buttresses. The avalanches feed the Kangshung Glacier, which drains into the deep gorge of the Arun River. Although the Kangshung side lies in Tibet, the climate and landscape with lush forests and glorious alpine meadows are similar to those in Nepal. Everything changes dramatically to the north where the light is more intense, the air is parched dry and the vegetation is sparse. After the winter winds, much of the North Face is bare rock, especially the famous Yellow Band which glows orange at sunset. These layers of sedimentary rock remind us that Everest originated from the bed of the ancient Tethys Sea long before India collided with Tibet to thrust up the greatest mountain barrier on earth. This face is framed by the West Ridge on the right, which rises from the Lhola, and by the North-East Ridge, on the left. The most prominent features on the North Face are the two gullies called the Great Couloir and the Hornbein Couloir. With the rise of commercial guiding, most ascents are made on only two routes – one in Nepal and the other in China.

I could not help becoming immersed in the history of Everest. I have to say that up until now, I had not paid much attention to it but, once I committed to the trip, I read several books. In 1924, British climber Edward Norton made a solo traverse of the Great Couloir without supplementary oxygen. He got to within 250 metres of the summit, setting an altitude record at that time. His ascent was remarkable, particularly considering that he was only equipped with nailed boots, an ice-axe and a few layers of woollen clothing. Four days later, George Mallory and Sandy Irvine disappeared attempting the crest of the North-East Ridge. They took oxygen and they may have climbed the formidable Second Step, a difficult rock barrier high on the ridge, to reach the summit, but it is unknown whether they summited or not. George Mallory's body has since been found in a tweed jacket with a receipt still in its pocket but sadly no sign of the camera which may have confirmed their success. Andrew Irvine's body is still somewhere on the mountain.

At the outbreak of the Second World War, Tibet closed its borders to all foreigners but Nepal opened its doors allowing Eric Shipton's 1951 team to reconnoitre the Khumbu Icefall and reach the Western Cwm. The following year, Sherpa Tenzing Norgay and his Swiss companion, Raymond Lambert, almost reached the summit by the South-East Ridge. It was Edmund Hillary who, with Tenzing Norgay, in 1953, made the historic first ascent. They were on John Hunt's British and Commonwealth Expedition, though Hillary was a New Zealander. Unless George Mallory and Andrew Irvine did summit in 1924, no Briton did until 1975. It was Dougal Haston and Doug Scott who completed the ascent of the much-tried South-West Face. Reaching the top at sunset, they spent the night on the South Summit, surviving the highest bivouac in history. For Doug Scott, Everest was the launch pad for a sequence of Himalayan ascents and the eventual completion of the seven summits.

Many more expeditions have summited since the first ascent. Notable ones include the American traverse of 1963 by Tom Hornbein and Willi Unsoeld. They climbed an indirect line up the West Ridge, then descended to the South Col. The South-West Face was climbed by Chris Bonington's meticulously organised expedition in 1975. The Russians climbed a harder, still unrepeated, line to the left in 1982. In 1979, the direct ascent of the very hard West Ridge 'Integrale' was achieved by a large Yugoslav team. However, the climb that really set the standard was by Reinhold Messner. In 1978, he made the first oxygen-free ascent of the mountain. Together with his Austrian climbing partner, Peter Habeler, he reached the summit in just over ten hours from the South Col. Even more remarkably, Habeler descended back to the South Col in just one hour. Two years later, Messner took another giant leap into the unknown with his solo oxygen-free ascent of the North Ridge and North Face. The ascent only became possible when Tibet was re-opened to foreigners. He was the only person on the mountain at the time, marking an historic first and only true solo ascent of the mountain.

Following Messner's lead, a small Australian team led by Tim Macartney-Snape climbed a direct line up the Great Couloir in 1984, summiting without oxygen. In 1986, the Swiss experts, Jean Troillet and Erhard Loretan astounded the world by climbing the Japanese Direct/Hornbein Couloir in just forty-two hours up and down. The Kangshung Face, deemed 'not climbable' by Mallory, was first climbed in 1983 by a large American expedition led by George Lowe along the spectacularly difficult lower buttress. In 1988, a four-man Anglo-American team made a new route further left, emerging at the South Col. They had been climbing without any Sherpa support or oxygen.

At 7,900 metres, the South Col is often referred to as the highest garbage dump in the world. Empty oxygen bottles, old tents, equipment, litter and even dead bodies make it look like a common landfill site. In an attempt to address the problem, the Nepalese government now charges a several-thousand-dollar environmental deposit to each expedition. The deposit is paid back after the liaison officer has confirmed that the expedition has removed its rubbish and equipment from the mountain. Compostable, burnable and other rubbish can be deposited in Namche Bazaar, however, used oxygen bottles, gas canisters and batteries have to be taken back to Kathmandu and exported out of the country. This is the theory, but whether it's put into practice is another matter entirely.

A similar system operates on the Tibetan side. However, the deposit is probably too small to have a positive effect. On both sides of the mountain, market forces apply. Visiting Western climbers rarely have the strength to carry down their own used oxygen bottles and other debris. They prefer to pay their Sherpa special bonuses to do the work for them. Litter on the mountain has become an aesthetic problem but, with the growing number of tourists to the Nepalese side, has caused more complex issues such as deforestation and erosion. These issues have arisen partly from local population pressures and also from the explosion of tourism in recent years. Visiting trekkers and climbers have an important role to play in preserving the mountain environment, by ensuring all their cooking is done on either gas or kerosene stoves, rather than using wood fires.

Even though records are being broken all the time, I hold the highest regard for the pioneer climbers. Besides the gear they wore, the food was not as good or as nutritious as it is now. Those using supplementary oxygen found it temperamental and unreliable. Most expeditions took a lot longer, climbers left the shores of England by boat and left their families for months. Climbers took longer on the mountain, staying at higher altitude instead of dropping down to allow their bodies to recover somewhat.

I had to get myself in the frame of mind for a possible thirteen-week trip. Cho Oyu had previously been the longest – a mere five weeks – and what a state I had returned in from that. I was looking to break a record and become the first Cornishman to climb Everest. What an honour it would be to leave a St Piran's flag on top of the world. I was also keen to raise some money for the British Heart Foundation. Despite working a sixty-hour week of mostly 4 a.m. starts, I exercised four times a week. At the time, I had no problem living that life but I had no time for socialising. I cocooned myself in a world of work and exercise, almost becoming a hermit. On top of that, after all my years of being cuddly, I now had to try and put on weight while training intensely. It wasn't easy but I did manage to put on half a stone.

When I first announced in the local papers what I was trying to achieve, the immediate response was, 'What, Base Camp?' I think people thought they would never see me again. The only negative comment I got was, 'He will not even reach Base Camp.' I tried to get on the local television but they turned me down abruptly which I chuntered at somewhat, bearing in mind some of the rubbish and trivia they report. During my last week before leaving for Everest, I spent the day with Mia, my niece, at London Zoo, on her third birthday. After looking at all the animals, she asked me what my favourite was. I replied 'the giraffe because he sees the top before anybody else'. As a reminder of our day, she bought me a small, soft giraffe as my mascot.

When I left at the end of March, from Heathrow, my mother was privately thinking, 'We may not ever see Edward again', as she later told me. My only trepidation was the unknown of the further 648 metres I would need to climb, if I got that far. With the aid of oxygen, I hoped to climb as high as Cho Oyu, after that I would be in the lap of the gods. I would give it my best shot, trusting my judgement if I had to abort a summit, but I was convinced I would return to Cornwall.

The route was very familiar indeed, a fork in the road led left to Everest and right to Cho Oyu. I had chosen to attempt the North-East Ridge from Tibet, not because of the cost but because of the Khumbu Icefall on the south side, the section which even the Tibetans and Nepalese dislike. They much prefer the north, even though it is considered harder but first I had to negotiate Zhangmu, Nyalam and Tingri again without becoming ill. We had already spent a week acclimatising in Lukla and going up the valley as far as Tengboche, preferring it to Kathmandu where there is always the risk of catching something. This was whilst the Chinese sorted out the personal and group visas to get into Tibet and on to the mountain. At Tengboche, we could see Everest to the south, and, to the right, we had a perfect picture of Ama Dablam, soaring nearly 7,000 metres, a breathtaking spire known as the Matterhorn of the Himalaya. It was once described by Edmund Hillary as 'not climbable', but it has been many times. I had to keep an open mind while travelling through this developing country, not everything is black and white. We were still waiting for the Chinese visas to come through.

I was interested in seeing if progress had been made since my previous trip in 2005. Signs were promising – a nice new building had been erected at the border crossing into Tibet. But looks were deceiving because once we were inside, it was just a lot of arm waving and shouting. There was no real organisation and we did lose some time as a couple of our members came under closer scrutiny and were frisked a little more thoroughly. Thankfully there was no problem and we were ushered out the other end like cows having just been milked. As we travelled through Zhangmu, there seemed to be no obvious changes, not until we got out and started winding our way up the mountains, like scenes out of *The Italian Job*. There had been road improvements to great cost, including a nice tarmac road with barriers along the edge. Consequently, though, other drivers took the improvements as license to drive recklessly, at speed. The Tata lorries came trundling down the road fully laden to the point of being overloaded, which caused them to lean when negotiating one of the many bends. The cynical side of me wondered how many of these lorries had a legitimate MOT certificate. At Pang-La Pass, at 5,150 metres, we stopped for a breather and a comfort break. There, we could see three 8,000-metre peaks, Cho Oyu, Makalu and Shishapangma, rising majestically. Standing there gazing, with the Tibetan prayer flags fluttering, I could feel the chill of the wind.

Dropping elevation to Nyalam, I was in for no more shocks. I was still coming to terms with the road improvements but it was still the same dirty, inhospitable place of six years before. The Nyalam Hotel was black and eerie with a hanging sign that creaked each time the wind blew. Unsurprisingly, the food was bad again and I resorted to eating from my six-kilogram bag of supplies. These supplies were what Cotswold had sponsored me with in return for a photo at the top if successful. The following day, after a rat-infested night in the hotel, we drove on to Tingri. There a new hotel had been built at the end of the main street. Wow, I thought, until I looked inside. The furniture was still wrapped up in clear plastic, like seat covers in a car. Smelling very cheap it was certainly not Ikea furniture. There was no hot water, it was just cold and brown. Already there were plaster cracks running down the walls like bad varicose veins. That night, I slept in my sleeping bag it was that cold. Each time a Tata lorry rumbled by on its way to Lhasa, it shook the hotel and its single-paned windows. It probably appears as though I am moaning over a couple days' hardship. To think, on Mallory's expedition he made a five-week pilgrimage just to get to Base Camp.

Thankfully, complete with visas, we made our way to Base Camp. The leader was Arnold Coster again, which I was pleased with. After my experiences on Cho Oyu, I realised there was no one else I would want to lead an expedition up the highest mountain in the world. I also realised when he first diagnosed my frostbite on Cho Oyu that as long as I kept away from infection, amputation would not be required. It came as no surprise to Arnold to hear I had made a full recovery from my ordeal. He had gained some extra pounds, was married to Maya Sherpa and had a baby daughter. Even though it had been six years, he remembered me and said I looked fitter, which was comforting to hear.

What was most pleasing was that we were a much smaller group – seven in total, the oldest being fifty-seven and the youngest twenty-six. Biff Palmer, a kidney surgeon from Texas was hoping to complete the seven summits, while Mark Quinn from Ireland was hoping to become the youngest Irishman to climb Everest. Frank Irnich, a German chiropractor, was attempting to summit for the second year running. He had got trapped at Camp 3 confined to the tent the previous year because he had frostbitten hands, while his buddy from Scotland went on to summit but never returned. His body was somewhere on the mountain up from Camp 3. Having achieved what I had, I no longer felt inferior, like I did when I turned up on Cho Oyu. I was putting together an impressive CV between Aconcagua, Denali and Cho Oyu. Arriving at Base Camp, at 5,200 metres, we helped unload the lorry full of kit and finished putting up tents. The combination of exercise and the cold wind sent my pulse racing to ninety-two beats per minute. Even with all the cardiovascular work I had done prior to the trip, my body was not prepared. I learned very quickly to do things slower. The early days at Base Camp were spent getting used to the environment, drinking lots of water and gazing up the valley at Everest. We could not put a limit on our liquid intake and we had to get into the habit of drinking regularly. At Base Camp and at Advanced, we had the sanctuary of our own tent and mattress. It was important to rest, so comfort was essential. We all shared a mess tent where, in the evenings, we watched films before hastily retreating to our own tents at 10 p.m. Because it was early season, the temperature plummeted to minus twenty-three degrees. Imagine what it was like on top.

After a few days, we moved up for the first time to Advanced Base Camp at 6,400 metres. Most of the equipment I needed higher up went on mules leaving me carrying a small rucksack. Samdien, our Tibetan cook, oversaw the loading of mules. It's amusing to see the haggling going on, bartering on equal loads and price. Scales make an appearance. Samdien was a good chef and was able to cook Western-style food to our liking. We learned that he was okay if he got his own way. If he was upset, the quality and quantity of our meals were not so good. If he wanted fresh vegetables or supplies, he got them.

We set off, taking the 'Magic Highway'. This journey took us across moraine through the ice pinnacles of the East Rongbuk Glacier to Everest's North Side. I found the air very thin at this height. Even though Everest lay forty kilometres to the West of Cho Oyu, the air was thinner. There was no doubt in my mind that I was going to be using oxygen and I would not worry about how much. Prior to the trip, I had thought maybe I would only use four bottles and sell a bottle. Now I completely dismissed the idea. I would use as much oxygen as was required. Advanced Base Camp was at the top of a steep incline so our tents were tighter together. At Advanced Base Camp, the oxygen levels were reduced to just forty-five per cent, which seemed preposterous as there was still over two kilometres of vertical ascent to climb before summiting. Spending about six nights there, we did different things each day. First, we put on all our climbing gear and practised on an ice wall near camp. From now on up, we would be on fixed ropes wearing climbing gear. We practised climbing up and abseiling down with the big mittens on. This was the hottest day yet, with blue skies and sunshine. Combined with the high altitude, after four hours I was knackered and glad to rest, taking on more liquid. From camp, looking up towards the summit, I noticed the wind sweeping cloud across the top – the classic banner cloud that is seen streaming from the summit of Everest. This phenomenon is often referred to as Everest 'smoking,' like a steam locomotive as is particularly noticeable at around 10 a.m. each day.

Before we went any further, we were invited to join the Tibetans and the Nepalese in their Puja blessing to pray for the safe return of everybody attempting the summit. The ceremony is traditional and much preparation is made for it. Wrapped up but shivering in the bitter wind, we were encouraged to place any items of equipment at the foot of the open-air altar and drink a libation called Tsampa, made of barley and fermented flour. If we had drunk enough of it, we could have become decidedly drunk.

On the final day before descending, I did a carry up to Camp 1, at 6,000 metres. The East Rongbuk headwall, which can be seen from camp, leads up to the North Col and along the intimidatingly exposed North Ridge. Slowly and carefully, I traversed up the mountain, using my ascender. The only crevasse we had to cross was at the foot of Camp 1. It was very unnerving at first, crossing a gorge, three aluminium ladder lengths long that flexed under our weight. It wasn't easy in my boots and crampons but if I got stage fright, my trip would have been curtailed before it had even started. All the cost, training and effort of getting there would have been in vain. Camp 1 was very much like a balcony looking down in the distance at Advanced. After making the cache, we returned for a much-needed rest at Base Camp. Everest is very much like a game of snakes and ladders, we didn't want to spend too long on a snake.

The weather was still volatile and we had already spent nearly two weeks at Base Camp. Arnold stressed the need for us to acclimatise adequately, as the season closes the second week in June. Groups only just arriving were not as likely to reach the summit. Now into the third week of May, there had been a dumping of snow, which showed just how unpredictable the weather could be; it should have been getting warmer and becoming settled. With plentiful rest and Samdien's cooking, we recuperated at the lower altitude until it was time to go up a second time. This time, after a night at Advanced, we were to push on to Camp 1 and stay three nights. I felt more conditioned at this altitude but I was still not pushing it. Arnold's relaxed, easy-going leadership, and taking our time, was paying dividends. Once at Camp 1, things became a bit harder. I had to share a tent and take responsibility for cooking and boiling water. Choosing somebody to share with was an important decision because climbing partners need to go at the same sort of speed and work together. So far Dominic and I were getting on quite well and we were keeping a steady rhythm going when we were on the move. Dominic Pickett was a Briton from Bristol. Aconcagua was the highest mountain he had climbed but, besides that, he had swum the Channel and had run several marathons. I was pleased he wanted to partner me because the other candidates, Mark and Frank, were a lot slower and did not seem to work together – one relied on the other to perform camp duties rather than sharing the workload. At Camp 1, we walked some of the route to Camp 2 along a steep ridge. This ridge offered no wind protection so it was essential we had down jackets and mittens on. We wore the down jackets whatever the weather. If the weather changed, there was not sufficient time to get our down out of our rucksacks and put it on before perishing in the elements. Arnold told us to go as far as possible and not to worry about getting to the rock band that led to Camp 2. I got as far as 7,500 metres, about the height of Camp 3 on Cho Oyu. That was the end of the second foray up the mountain and I was pleased with my progress. It was also the end of the acclimatisation programme. The next time up, it would be for real.

CHAPTER 10

PUSHING FOR SUMMIT

I've had it. Anybody who sees me in a boat
has my permission to shoot me.

— SIR STEVE REDGRAVE

Base Camp was a welcome sight. Finally, the springtime weather had arrived, we just needed to wait for four to five days of settled conditions to give us a good chance of getting to the top. Arnold was pleased with the way things had gone and he said that we were a reasonably quick group. We also had to wait for the Chinese to fix fresh ropes higher up. Every year, each expedition pays into the Chinese Association for tasks such as this. Old ropes are still in place from previous years but they fray at the pitons, making them unsafe. Part of the reason things were slow was that an American had planted a 'Free Dalai Lama' flag down at the border crossing, which was threatening to have serious consequences due to the sensitive politics in the region. In the past, it has been known for the army to close the mountain down. This would have ruined my chances completely. My last email home was full of despondency and uncertainty. Up until now, things had gone brilliantly, bearing in mind how things were on Cho Oyu. I felt I still had a lot to give and I had adapted to Samdien's cooking. It felt as though the half a stone I had put on for the trip was still there. I had hardly touched the food I had brought with me because Samdien was cooking Western-style food. Thankfully things settled down at the border and the necessary work was carried out higher up. Closing down the mountain would result in the Chinese losing a large source of income.

At Base Camp, I walked around a graveyard called Memorial Hill. I was well-aware I would see bodies higher up. It is a known fact that once stricken climbers go off their feet, they are left behind. In the past, guides and Sherpas tried to bring bodies down but in reality it was just too diffi-cult. Also it meant putting their lives at risk even more and the clients they are looking after. Instead memorials were built at Base Camp instead. The most elaborate one I saw was for George Mallory and Andrew Irvine but the latter's body is still somewhere on the mountain. Frank, one of our team members, was hoping to take with him pictures of his Scottish friend, who had previously died on the mountain, and take summit photos back to his family on the Isle of Skye, as they felt they had never said goodbye. He was going to build a memorial down at Base Camp – an idea that I thought was very touching and caring. The two climbers had only known each other a few weeks but they had formed such a strong bond, it was as though they had been friends for years. One night we spent a bit lower down at the Rongbuk monastery, the sacred threshold to the north side of Everest at 5,000 metres. It may seem as though it was not very advan-tageous to drop down at this point, but I wanted to feel in top condition for the final onslaught.

One afternoon, all the groups at Base Camp were invited to join a Russian team, called the 'Seven Summits'. I was wary of catching some-thing at this crucial stage and chose not to eat any of the food on offer but I did chat to some of the members who, like us, were ready to go up. One guy I met was John Delaney, who was forty-two and from Ireland. He was attempting the summit for the second time but, even more astonishingly, his wife was about to go into labour with their second child. Before the party got too wild, I made a hasty retreat to my tent. If I was to celebrate, I would do it when I came down.

A weather window came through around the 21st of May. All 125 climbers at Base Camp were attempting to head back up the mountain to push for the summit. Setting off from Camp 1 on the 19th, I would be on oxygen all the way up and back again. We were using the Poisk system, manufactured in St Petersburg, Russia. The cylinders were 19 inches long and 4.25 inches in diameter, weighing two pounds. On two-litres-per-minute flow, they lasted approximately six-and-a-half hours. I had it on setting two while moving and I turned it back to point five when resting. I never carried more than one bottle at a time. From Camp 1, the four guides had two bottles, albeit operating on a reduced setting. It was then I started to appreciate the physiology of these people. One year, Lakpa Sherpa left north Base Camp, Tibet, summited and was down on the south side Base Camp, in Nepal, in just twenty-two hours.

It is a scientific fact that the body does not rest at altitude so at 7,000 metres my recovery was limited. I think I still had reasonable rest and the soft snow underneath helped considerably but things were decidedly difficult now most of the team was suffering with sleep deprivation, loss of appetite and dehydration. Yes I was on supplementary oxygen but I still had 1,848 metres to go. I had been fortunate enough not to have contracted an illness up until now. The half stone I put on in Cornwall while training and my fluid intake at Base Camp would prove invaluable.

Leaving the North Col, I made my way up and on to the intimidating, exposed North Ridge. Even though it was overcast with low cloud and no wind, I still had my down on in case the weather changed. I also wore high-UV sunglasses to shield my eyes from the continuing glare of the snow and I kept my head bowed. Once on the ridge, the first part of the walk was comfortable because I had been up to 7,500 metres before and I had the added bonus of oxygen. From then on, it became steeper and harder. I went into a rockier band and found myself using the ice-axe as a walking stick. At times, my leg was at a ninety-degree right angle. The ropes were still there but they were woven around the bare rocks, having been blown by the wind. It was difficult to navigate over the meandering rope in crampons. The blasting wind had revealed even more bare rocks on the north side. At times, it would have been a lot easier without crampons but taking them off and putting back them on again would have wasted vital energy. The snow was no longer soft but hard with an icy sheen to it and my crampons crunched as they dug in.

Quite a way into the rock band, I started to see the tents of Camp 2. They were not situated in rows or definite sites, but pitched anywhere remotely flat with rocks so that guy ropes could be lashed round them. Some ropes were straining at the leash because it was particularly windy. If I twanged them, it would have been like plucking a taut string on a violin. Finding a spot, Dominic and I now had to put up our tent. Unlike at Camp 1, tents left here would be lucky to survive one night, let alone a week. Now Dominic and I had to communicate clearly. This was our sanctuary from the elements. Losing the tent would mean kissing goodbye to a summit bid. Hollering above the wind, we pitched our tent, cowering so as not to get caught in the blast. If the wind had caught right, our tent would have looked like a sail on a boat and would have surely been a goner. We battled manfully, tying the ropes around rocks and tamping pegs into the hard ground. Bundling Dominic into the tent, I said I would go and get some snow for the night. Because there were more bare patches, I had to go further to dig for snow with my ice-axe.

Thus far, I had managed to keep my hands free from abrasions, any I received now would be fatal. Open wounds, even if they are only a mere cut, do not heal in this environment. Using the tent bag and a stuff sack,

I crammed as much snow in as possible. Once in the confines of the tent, I did not leave until morning. It was like camping on the edge of an eroding cliff at Seaton in Cornwall. We had a spectacular view above the clouds at 7,800 metres but the environment was so inhospitable. I settled as comfortably as I could, only having a thin Karrimat on top of little pieces of rock. Dominic had started boiling the first lot of water, the stove swung in the vestibule of the tent, but he was careful not to let it catch alight. In the high altitude, the water took longer to boil. We used water tablets to safeguard against infection. Settling down, we listened to the wind howling and tossing. Lack of oxygen and an uncomfortable bed combined for a very restless night.

Just as we had witnessed at Advanced Base Camp, the morning of the 20th of May brought better weather so we began our 500-metre journey to Camp 3. Soon after we reached 7,900 metres, we entered the Death Zone. It is exactly that; even with the use of supplementary oxygen, the body is not designed to live at that altitude. The red blood cells produced initially to cope with the reduced levels of oxygen begin to die. The name of the game changed from that point and the clock was ticking. Whereas before we walked slowly to become acclimatised, now we had to get the job done as quickly as possible and get back down. Moving quickly was a false economy – we convinced ourselves we were moving faster but actually we were doing things slower. Simple tasks took longer and left us out of breath. Airline passengers, if exposed to the air at this height, would lapse into a coma within minutes. Yet it felt safer here without the Khumbu Icefall to contend with. Instead there was more bare rock and there were three steps to negotiate before we got to the final pyramid, the jewel at the top of the crown. Climbers on the north side of Everest are in the Death Zone for at least one day and some are there longer – this is why it is considered to be harder than the south side overall.

It was a steep clamber into Camp 3, at 8,300 metres, the highest camp in the world. The tents occupied the smallest of spaces, perched precariously on snow platforms no bigger than car bonnets. One tent was erected on a ledge, which was almost precipice-like. If caught in the wind, a climber and the tent could be blown away like rag dolls. We had to fight for a pitch, it was a 'free for all'. The camp was particularly busy with everybody going for the summit that night. I had already used a new oxygen bottle at Camp 2 so this left me with three remaining bottles. Two went with me up the mountain and I left the fifth in camp. After erecting the tent and collecting snow, Dominic and I dived into the shelter. Shortly we were joined by our Tibetan guide, Tenji Sherpa, our Guardian Angel. Even though he had worked tirelessly on our behalf, he now had the extra burden of accompanying us up to the summit and back again. Gyalje, Jinpa, Lakpa and Tenji had been working higher up the mountain whilst we were recuperating down at base camp. Establishing the higher camps and carrying the equipment up. Thirty-five bottles of client oxygen plus two bottles each for their own use. You start to appreciate the physiology of these people. Cheerfully, he set about lighting the stove and boiling water. At this height, a simple mug of tea took forty-five minutes to make. At these temperatures if water is thrown into the air, it freezes before hitting the ground. However, using stoves is risky because compressed oxygen can cause a deadly explosion.

Tenji pulled out some dried noodles and biscuits and offered them to us expectantly, with a beaming smile. Transfixed, we both stared back at him, zombie-like, with our masks resolutely fixed over our mouths and noses. How could he be so happy and vibrant with energy? Stirring ourselves, we did eat some dried biscuits and shared some noodles. It was an effort to digest these offerings and they certainly would not replace the calories we burnt. Feeling somewhat replenished, I set about organising what I needed on summit night. I planned not to take off my rucksack because this would use up valuable energy and I may have become constrained in tangled oxygen tubing. I did not want to disturb my oxygen flow as this was my lifeline. My camera and spare batteries went into my down jacket, along with a photo of my family. Dominic's camera had fallen foul of the altitude so he was relying on me for pictures. Besides that, I had a St Piran's flag and a Cotswold bag, a token photo for helping out with my food for the trip. I also attached my mascot, Mia's giraffe, on to the zipper of my down jacket.

Given the large volume of people, it was important to not get stuck behind traffic going up the mountain. To avoid the risk of bottlenecks, which are notorious around the Second Step, the times between groups leaving were staggered. Overcrowding is a problem as is blind ambition from many, not always experienced, climbers. This leads to deaths on the mountain, like the 1996 Everest disaster when over the 10th and 11th of May eight people died. Prior to the spring of 2014 this was the worst recorded disaster on the mountain. Growing numbers of people on the mountain only increases the risk. Even the most skilful, high-altitude climbers can perish. If turnaround times on the summit are not obeyed, disaster is inevitable. But it's not just the volume of people increasing the bottlenecks on the mountains, more accurate weather forecasts have led climbers to time their attempts on the same few days each year. Arnold instructed us to move quite quickly and he relayed through radio that we would be leaving at 10 p.m.

Some people slept but I chose not to. I figured trying to sleep would not be beneficial, considering where I was. I was feeling focused, motivated and, with the aid of oxygen, I had energy to burn. With all my past experiences, I trusted myself to turn around if something went wrong but I felt I still had a lot more to give. It is the mind that needs to stay strong, even when the body tires. With the weather forecasted, would I be given the opportunity of my shot at Everest?

Outside our tent, I had trouble fixing my crampons on to my boots. Whether it was nerves, excitement or that I was too cold, I don't know but it took longer than normal. I had used up valuable energy and I had not even stepped out on to the trail. About half an hour into our walk, following the trail of headlamps, mine began to flicker. It couldn't be the batteries because I was sure I had replaced them at Camp 3. I decided to climb on under the clear, starry moonlit sky, picking up the heels of Dominic in front of me. As we got into a steady rhythm, we overtook slower groups, where convenient. If we got caught behind people, we risked our bodies cooling down, leading to hypothermia, shutdown and death. Once on the ridge, we tackled the three steps now well into the Death Zone. The First and Second Steps are the main difficulties on this side of the mountain. Fixed ropes safeguard ascents and descents. Before tackling the First Step, we passed a landmark called Green Boots Cave, at 8,500 metres. This sad site is a well-known landmark, named after a dead Indian climber who still lies curled in the rocky alcove, clad in green high-altitude boots. A few spent oxygen bottles had been left on the ledge. The First Step was fairly easy and we negotiated it quickly. The only stopping point was Mushroom Rock at 8,549 metres, where I exchanged my partly used oxygen bottle for a fresh one. Neither Dominic nor I took off our rucksacks in an effort to conserve valuable energy. Our rucksacks also acted as a windbreak against the cold – not that I was feeling cold. Tenji had been carrying our oxygen bottles so he would have a lighter load from here on up. Peering at him behind the oxygen mask, I imagined him still smiling those pearly whites. If a climber was fortunate enough to reach this point, he or she knew there was at most two hours to go before the summit.

On a fresh bottle of oxygen, it was time for me to tackle the notorious Second Step at 8,610 metres. Vertical climbing at extreme altitude was exhausting. An aluminium ladder, which looks like it has come from a do it yourself store, has been secured to the rock. This was where Noel Odell last saw Mallory and Irvine, in 1924, 'going strongly for the top'. There is still debate as to whether they reached the summit. Could they have climbed this vertical Second Step, I wonder if we will ever know for sure? I was looking forward to climbing those significant steps, steeped in the history of the earliest attempts on Everest in the 1920s and 1930s. On our approach, I could see people on the Second Step. Tentatively, peering up through my snow glasses, I waited at the bottom for them to come down. I wondered what time had they set off for summit. I silently prayed that there was not a queue of people behind the brow of the hill. Thankfully there was not and as soon as the last foot was off the ladder, mine was on it. I needed no second invitation to begin my ascent but I had to be careful not to become entangled in the array of ropes bestrewn on the floor. I felt bloated, like the Michelin Man, in my down jacket and salopettes. Once up and safely on my way again, I breathed a sigh of relief. I had been particularly concerned about being bottlenecked on the Second Step. The final step, at 8,690 metres, was fairly easy, it was a big lump of rock where we rolled our bodies along the right side.

We were now at the foot of the pyramid that sits on top of the lump that is Everest. To start with, there was more climbing involved. People ask if Everest is technically difficult to climb. It is not but there is some scrabbling and tight gullies, which were not easy to navigate with the clothing we had on because it snags and tears easily. At times, I wished I wasn't wearing crampons while walking across the bare rock but taking them off was not a feasible option. The crampon points made an eerie scraping noise like fingernails going down a blackboard. It felt as though we were making good progress. If I had to guess, it was the early hours of the morning and dawn would be breaking soon. Not long after, there was a group stopped with a climber clearly in distress. It was the Seven Summits group and, unbeknown to me, it was John Delaney who was suffering, the guy I had been talking to only a few days earlier. After Tenji offered him the medical supplies he was carrying, we went towards the summit. It was starting to get busier now, with traffic going both ways. I had the feeling it was not far: 'Keep going Ed', I urged myself.

On the final climb up to the summit, I saw a familiar face peering down at me. It was Arnold pointing off to my right, with his face mask off, saying, 'Look Ed, there's the summit. You've done it.' Not quite, I thought, but I nodded and held my thumb up, my face cocooned in my oxygen mask sucking every drop like the last dregs of a banana milkshake. There was little margin for error on the final slope. On the left, was a huge plunge down to certain death. On the right was a slope that went down like a ramp and off the edge of the mountain. I could see people on top, jubilant and triumphant in success.

It was around 7 a.m. on 21 May 2011 that I stood on top of the world. I saw plenty of people unclipping and jumping about. What were they celebrating? I thought. Yes it was a fine, clear morning, around minus thirty-five degrees, with a wind chill of ten-to-fifteen miles per hour, but the weather could change at any time. I was going to stay clipped in and not celebrate. Dominic was shouting, 'Ed take photos, take photos.' I dug in my jacket for the camera and pulled it out. Turning it on, I saw the red battery light flashing. The altitude had got to my camera as well as my head torch. I prayed the spare batteries would be all right. Thankfully it was flashing half so I got on and took photos before it too succumbed to the altitude. There was no orderly queue, it was a free for all; people clambered for summit shots. I handed my camera to Tenji and he set about taking photos of Dominic, me, my Cotswold bag and my proud St Piran's flag. There was no St Piran's flag on the ground. We could not help getting other people and rucksacks in the shots. Looking at Dominic, I could see hoar frost in his beard and his cheeks were puffy with the altitude. At almost 8,850 metres, large aircraft, with passengers comfortably sitting in a pressurised cabin, would probably be flying less than 2,000 metres above us.

On the summit, there is only a third of the oxygen available at sea level. My giraffe was solid ice and stuck to my coat. 'Giraffes don't like the severe cold,' I thought. I will be able to answer that in a pub quiz in years to come. Satisfied with my shots, I proudly laid my St Piran's on the altar of Everest, next to the other flags and mementoes. Still fixed on the ropes, I walked over and peered down towards the South Side. I could see climbers coming up over the Hillary Step towards the summit. Walking a bit further over to the right, careful not to go over the edge, I bowed my head. Staring up at me was the wide plateau of Cho Oyu, my summit of six years previously. I always appreciate views and boy I had one now: the sheer range of the Himalaya and among them, somewhere, some of the other 8,000ers. The burnished plains of Tibet were to the north and the majestic peaks of lush foothills of Nepal were to the south. After climbing for nine hours, we had only twenty minutes on the summit, which hardly seemed worth it but such is the draw of Everest. It is a honey pot and will always attract climbers who want to stand on top of the world. Nowadays the climbing might be less technical, with ropes fixed to help progress up and down but it is still a worthwhile climb. The dangers of avalanche, extreme weather, frostbite and high altitude will always remain. Even though today a climber can buy a place on an organised, sometimes, guided expedition, Everest should not be underestimated. The ascent is still a deadly challenge. Now it was time to go down. If the weather was stable, it was possible to remain on the summit for longer but our good weather window was closing. The lenticular clouds we had seen lower down on the mountain would soon be upon us, bringing very high winds. Stuffing my camera in my down jacket, I turned my attention to the descent. Even in daylight, this was when the majority of accidents happen. Fatigue, sleep deprivation, lack of food, dehydration, the altitude and the euphoria of summiting all contribute to the risk of accident. I had to be on top of my game more than ever because, quite simply, as the old adage says, 'no summit is recorded unless the climber returns'. In my mind I was only halfway.

Starting down, we just used our karabiners and our ice-axes. There were still plenty of people coming up whom we courteously allowed to pass. Further on, I saw my first dead body. It was John Delaney, the man I had met at Base Camp. It was the first of about eight I saw, all in different states of desecration. I remember stepping over a torso lying horizontally across the path, like the hollow of a tree in the woods in Cornwall. Another was crouched behind rocks, perhaps sheltering or taking a pee. I wondered where Andrew Irvine's body was. Whenever I saw a body, it spurred me on and kept my brain active, or else I could have ended up sacrificed to Everest. I plodded on down, negotiating the three steps. Thankfully there was no bottleneck on the Second Step, though it was harder getting on to it. Once off the ridge, I could start to see Camp 3 in the distance. Dominic was moving quicker than me, leaving Tenji and me bringing up the rear. Eventually I made it into Camp 3, six hours after summiting. It had been a fifteen-hour round trip.

After we had rested, the idea was to descend further. Dominic packed up and began his descent but I staggered a few steps and Lakpa hauled me back saying, 'You go down tomorrow.' I was exhausted, I needed to rest, but how could I rest trapped in the Death Zone? That night, there were four of us in a tent, two being Frank and Mark. Frank had got to the summit, taking photographs of his comrade from a year before with him. Mark had also reached the summit where he filmed a short video for a crisp commercial to be aired back in Ireland. Our tent sloped horizontally down the hill. With the four of us and our oxygen, it was cosy but uncomfortable, the gravel and small rocks probed into my back. My mind was still pretty active and sleep was fitful throughout the night. I was just hoping my weary body was rested enough to go down the next day. As I snatched at sleep, I listened to what was going on around me. The most dramatic change was the weather and the wind. By morning the wind had turned into a storm, travelling at forty to fifty miles per hour, sweeping across Camp 3 and above. Nobody was making a summit attempt. People were scarpering down the mountain. I was doing the same on my last bottle of oxygen, which had eight hours maximum left in it. I had spent nearly forty-eight hours in the Death Zone; it was time to get out. Setting off, my target was Camp 2. I cowered each time I came to change direction at a rock, removing my karabiner and fixing on a new line. There was no way I was going to be swept off this mountain. I was on my own, Tenji and the guides were clearing the camp behind me, collecting any empty bottles. The guides earned extra dollars for every empty bottle brought down in an effort to clean up the mountain. From what I witnessed, they still have a very long way to go. Fifty dollars to you or me might not sound very much but to them it is a small fortune. On this Everest trip, they would earn up to six months wages. I do not begrudge them a penny of it, putting their lives at risk with their families at home worried. However, it is a way of life for them and the risk is accepted. As nobody was coming up, I made good progress and soon reached Camp 2, which was spread out among the rocks. Not bothering to find our tent, I dived into an abandoned tent to make a quick adjustment and have bite to eat. I limited the amount of time I spent in the tent because if I allowed myself to get too comfy I would not move again. It occurred to me that our tent may have been blown off like a kite, together with my few supplies. I realised how much rubbish is left on Everest. There were abandoned tents, cookers, fuel and oxygen bottles strewn around camp. Most of the rubbish comes from private groups – people who will never go back again. If the bigger commercial companies left rubbish they would not get visas for the mountain the following year.

Out of the rocky band on the North Ridge, the weather had changed. The wind had dropped and, during my rapid descent, it was actually quite pleasant. I now had my next goal in sight – Camp 1. Reaching Camp 1, there was more shelter as the tents were packed tightly together. Again, I did not stop for too long because I wanted to get down the East Rongbuk headwall. Lakpa was already there, such was his speed. He was waiting there until the last guide came down, monitoring everybody coming off the mountain like a teacher on a school trip. Waving Lakpa goodbye, I made good progress down the headwall and was soon trudging towards Advanced Base Camp. In my head, I was starting to think of things I was missing at home. After eight weeks on camp food and boiled water, with a hint of kerosene in it, my palate was craving change. I fancied a traditional roast beef dinner and a glass of red wine. It would be a few more days before I got either of those.

As I looked up, I could see two people coming towards me. Two cook boys had been sent out to look for me. They took off my rucksack and beckoned me to sit. Needing no second invitation, I sat down and one of them produced a red can of cola, like a rabbit out of a hat. I do not usually drink fizzy drinks but it was the sweetest, most sugary thing he could offer me. It was the energy boost I had been looking for. They did not carry my rucksack for me but with renewed vigour I set off again. As I staggered zombie-like through the sprawl of Advanced Base Camp, fellow climbers just off the path stared at me acknowledging that I was looking weary and exhausted. As I picked my way through, I felt as though I was in a scene from *Saving Private Ryan*, returning from battle. On reaching our mess tent, I took my rucksack and crampons off and pulled the zipper up. Peering in, I saw some of the others dining round the table. The first person to get up was Arnold who looked at me and said, 'Well done, Ed.

The first Cornishman to climb Everest.' That was the first time I thought about what I had achieved, having been so wrapped up in returning safely. I ate and slept extremely well that night.

Waking up feeling refreshed, I packed up and was keen to get down to Base Camp, bypassing the intermediate camp completely. Six hours later I was down and, after a very quick shower and having put on reasonably fresh clothes after eight weeks on the mountain, I was back in my tent. It was time to make the phone call home to my family. I had already decided Base Camp was the place to do it. Some people phone from the summit but, if I had been lucky enough to have had a signal, do you think my family would have been any less anxious for my safety? I had enough to contend with, don't you think? They already knew I had summited but were, nevertheless, thrilled to hear from me and I assured them I had no frostbite this time but I did have a dry cough and a sore throat, parched from the use of oxygen. We had all summited, which Arnold had had high hopes for. I felt sorry for Mark; his achievement had been tainted because John Delaney had died. The cause of death was put down as heart related but how can anyone make an assessment like that at this height? If somebody dies, the company is supposed to make first contact with the bereaved. John's wife had found out after delivering their second child. I discovered that he had been giving away his personal possessions prior to going for the final summit push. With all that was going on with him, was he in the right frame of mind to climb Everest? Should he have been on the mountain at all?

I was pleased for Frank. He was a good man. He had suffered frostbite to the feet this year but had summited. Biff had completed the seven summits at fifty-seven years of age. Getting into the Land Cruiser for the journey back, I turned to look at the mountain for the final time. Everest had briefly smiled and allowed me to wipe my feet, step on to her throne and kneel at her altar. 'Thank you' I said, 'for allowing me in.'

CHAPTER 11

THE GOAL OF SEVEN SUMMITS

The quest to reach the highest point on every continent.

'You look as though you have been to the Bahamas!' my mother exclaimed, a week after I had summited Everest, as I was pushing my baggage through the arrivals on a bank holiday weekend in May. I turned to her and said, 'Well I have been on holiday for nine weeks.' All my family were there, greeting me with a banner saying, 'You did it Everest Ed.' Even my nieces were there, Mia and six-month-old Jessica, dressed in pyjamas and desperately trying to stay awake in my arms to take in the momentous occasion. My mother was expecting me to come back drawn, gaunt and bedraggled like I did from Cho Oyu but, in fact, I was looking well and had a glow about me. I had only lost half a stone, which I had put on especially for the trip. On average, people lose up to two stones on Everest. I think it was the combination of experience, good food, oxygen and being fitter. Climbers could easily panic and become claustrophobic with the mere thought of attempting Everest. It is important to have a strategic approach and tackle the mountain in small stages. It becomes a war of attrition to slay Chomolungma.

Let me reiterate, Everest had been no cake walk. Even with the use of supplementary oxygen it is only putting off the prospect of death if exposed in that environment too long. Just because you use oxygen it does not give you an automatic pass to the top. I couldn't have done it without Arnold, his approach was very relaxed and reassuring. He quietly cajoled us up the mountain like a father figure. On reflection, I had only walked for around twelve days. The rest of the time was spent at Advanced Base and Base Camp, watching films and reading. Cho Oyu had been harder for me, but I could not come home and say that without sounding pompous and arrogant. Any 8,000-metre peak is hard but attempting one without oxygen raises that difficulty further. In hindsight, I should have used oxygen but I had convinced myself I could do it without. I was severely tested and pushed to the limits. I had the mental strength and tenacity to get me through even the unforeseen events. Everybody is different in body and mind. A person can have the fittest body but if moments of weakness enter the mind it can spread like wildfire and prevent further progress. There are some purists like Reinhold Messner – and George Mallory before he died – who believe using oxygen is cheating. But would you attempt Everest without mountaineering boots or proper down mittens? Even a lump of sugar in your lukewarm tea could be considered artificial aid because all these things would undoubtedly increase your chances of summiting. There is talk about putting aluminium ladders up the Hillary Step to try and get people up and down quicker, like the ladder up the Second Step on the north side, is this not an artificial aid?

As I made my way back to Cornwall, I spent a couple of days at the Royal Cornwall Show in Wadebridge on the British Heart Foundation stand talking about my experiences and showing photos. I met with both young and old people with heart conditions and told them I had raised just under four thousand pounds for the charity. This gave me a great sense of pride and achievement at what I had just accomplished and sharing it with those less fortunate was humbling. The show has a strong agricultural theme and I managed to upstage the prize-winning bull. I got on the front page of the paper, relegating him to the inner pages. But I didn't have as much luck on the television front. Local broadcasters still claimed that because I did not have video footage, they could not do a piece on me. I have to say, it did irritate me, after all, I had just made history. It highlighted their lack of understanding of the impracticality of carrying camera equipment in such difficult terrain. I had the photos and certificate as evidence. Hiring a Sherpa to carry the extra weight for me was not within my budget and I had enough battery issues as it was without the burden of a video recorder. What if my mind had been distracted while filming and I had misplaced a step? I may have fallen to my death. I went with the intention of summiting and not having to go back again. This trip alone had cost me about 20,000 pounds.

Going back to work was easy, I spent the first day being congratulated. Many thought they would never see me again. The post could well have been late that day. In celebration Mum and Dad held a house warming for their friends and raised 800 pounds for my cause. Never one much for over doing the back slapping and high fives I already had a new focus.

During the flight home, I had begun thinking about what I was going to do next and I came up with a new objective – to complete all seven summits. Everest had been my fifth, leaving me with Kosciuszko in Australia, and Vinson in Antarctica. There is also the Carstensz Pyramid in West Papua, Indonesia (also in the continent of Australasia). Closed to tourists for years, it vies with Kosciuszko for inclusion in the seven summit list. Out of them all, it is the most technically difficult to climb and is more expensive to get to than Australia. Australia was to be my next destination. I planned to go out on a big one – Antarctica.

My expedition to Everest had created new opportunities for me to deliver talks and presentations. This was one of the aspects I found most enjoyable during my seven summits experience. In comparison, Brown Willy was a mere speck of dust. My first talk was at my dad's Zetland Lodge.

Armed with a projector and some personal equipment I had used on the trip, I set about holding the audience's attention. Just before starting, the Grand Master asked me to make sure I was finished before dinner. No added pressure on my first talk then. It went well and since then I have delivered countless other talks to rotaries, women's institutes, men's groups and Landrake Young Farmers. I was using my public-speaking practice from all those years ago to good effect. On finishing one of my talks at the WI a lady announced, 'You'll have to come back again when you've completed the seven.'

More recently, at a talk I gave to the Stoke Climsland WI, one lady asked a potentially awkward question: 'What about a Mrs Buckingham? What does she think about all these trips? Is there any love? Are you active?' Pausing to gather myself for the reply I thought that is more than one question. Replying I said, 'There is no Mrs Buckingham but I have a girlfriend. Perhaps if she had been here tonight you could have asked her direct. But in answer to your main question, yes I think I am still very much active.' You can imagine it brought the house down and was a good way to end the evening.

I chuckle after some talks. During one I did in the Elms nursing home, I had to stop several times for the residents to go to the toilet or go for a smoke. But it's always nice when somebody says something positive like, 'One day it would be nice to write a book.' I generally ask whether anybody has got any questions at the end and that amuses me. I get the regular ones like, 'What happens to the dead bodies?' and 'What do you do if you want to go to the toilet?' but, from time to time, I do get some new ones which is nice. In truth, Everest is such a broad subject that I have to limit the length of time for the presentation or else some audiences would fall asleep. Nothing prepares me for the audience's reaction or the range of questions people ask. Without sounding pompous or arrogant, my talks have gone down well and many venues have invited me back to speak again.

At the beginning of 2012, I joined a running club right on my doorstep, Moorlands Lane, the home of Saltash Rugby Club and the Tamar Trotters; the club I was pushed to play rugby for all those years ago. I had achieved all this and now I was joining people who could potentially make me fitter. I enjoyed it immediately. It reminded me of Young Farmers with a bit of running and some socialising. The main difference being that Young Farmers finishes when a member turns twenty-six, whereas there is no age limit in the running club. I met a range of people who had experienced all sorts, whereas in Young Farmers everybody was still 'wet behind the ears'. Tension and emotions do boil over on occasion but there is nothing wrong in showing emotion when preparing for a race. Race day is the release of all that effort. Upon joining the club, I bumped into old friends I had known right back in primary school, Phil Pollard and Scott and Jane Ivins. Our lives have since been very different but it's as though we have gone full circle, ending back on the same doorstep.

One of the first people I met was a Welshman called Mark Evans. It is fair to say that when he goes out it's not just to the local shop for a paper, it's for hours. On listening to me he said, 'You'll never get much out of running after all that you have achieved.' I have often thought about that comment. It is probably true to some degree, but I have enjoyed what I have done so far. I seem to revel in the marathons and the three ultras which are about preparing the mind for the long haul, but I have also taken part in several half marathons. I find half marathons and the shorter distances are a different proposition altogether. It's almost expected that a runner will move at a faster pace and I find the pressure is intensified. Approaching a marathon or an ultra requires a very different mindset. Set off at a relentless pace and there is a risk of burn-out and underachievement.

I also met Jane Bremner who likes the marathons and ultras. Jane seems to steadily go through the race and finish strongly. This is testament to her planning and training regime. Building up stamina takes months, even years, of training. Not many days go by where Jane is not running, cycling or doing some gym work. Truly a source of inspiration, Jane regularly picks up category age prizes in events. This must give her huge satisfaction and sets the benchmark for people like myself and others. I like to try and beat her. Not so that I can gloat or celebrate but to pit my wits against her. I have a tremendous amount of respect for Jane. I, however, seem to run quicker in the middle and then struggle towards the end. I need to adopt my mountain approach to running. As well as improving my fitness, I need to develop a race strategy and put it into practice. I don't think I will improve just by pounding the unforgiving streets. Dare I say it, but, after having avoided it for years, I think using the gym to work on different muscles and my core strength could improve my running. I need to play around with different strategies to find out what works for me, while balancing my career and home life. On the marathons and ultras, I try and take fluid on board, just as I do when I'm in the mountains, but, actually, runners do not drink very much. At the end of a couple of marathons, my stomach has felt like a washing machine.

For the humble person off the street, sport at any level is hard to maintain integrated with our hectic daily lives. Juggling work, family life and regular training schedules. For this George Prewett deserves a special mention. In October 2015 he competed in the world triathlon event at Kona in Hawaii. What a fantastic experience and achievement. To get to that level of competition takes a tremendous amount of dedication and hours spent working in the gym, swimming, running or cycling. Besides that think about the money it has cost for the equipment and events entered in competition with direct rivals. Added to that George has juggled with shifts in the dockyard and having a young son to bring up. George is a credit to himself, family, friends and as a Tamar Trotters representative. But running for me plays second fiddle to completing the seven summits, the sixth of which was Kosciuszko, at 2,228 metres in January 2013.

Kosciuszko lies in the Snowy Mountains of New South Wales, part of the Great Dividing Range. It straddles the state borders of Victoria and New South Wales, sitting bang in the middle of Sydney and Melbourne, about 280 miles from each. Australia has no glaciated mountains and Kosciuszko is little more than high moorland with no mountaineering interest. In the words of Dick Bass, it is 'a walk in the park'. It is unlikely to appear in any commercial expedition operator's brochure but for many years it has proved a popular holiday destination. Were it not for its status as a continental summit, the world's mountaineers would not have heard of it. On a good day, T-shirts and shorts, trainers and a good supply of suntan lotion are required. It definitely has the atmosphere of a family outing, making it a very different proposition to Everest.

It is best to climb the mountain in summer, from November to February, when the weather is fine, but March and April can be good. However, attempting the mountain in winter can be a challenge; snow is common, as are blizzards and sometimes deadly avalanches. Even though Kosciuszko does not compare to Everest, it cannot be taken lightly. The Kosciuszko plateau reminded me of the Scottish Highlands, especially once you climb out of the pine and eucalyptus forest. In the skies there are ravens and falcons. The higher plateau is home to small rodents, snakes and spiders – some of them poisonous. Lower down, a lucky observer might glimpse an echidna (like a large hedgehog) or a brumby (a wild horse). Aboriginals would have most certainly climbed Kosciuszko but it wasn't until 1824 that it was seen by white men. In 1839, the Polish explorer Sir Paul Edmund de Strzelecki explored the remote south-eastern part of Australia climbing to the summit of Kosciuszko on 15 February 1840.

The route I took was from Charlotte's Pass, 1,840 metres from the car park, which is reached by the sealed Kosciuszko Road. Beyond there is a gravel four-wheel-drive track. It is prohibited to vehicles, but not mountain bikes. Along the way it passes Seaman's Hut, an old emergency refuge and the highest building in Australia. It is dedicated to Laurie Seaman who died of hypothermia in 1928. The track finally circles around the back, like a spiral, to the summit, passing the highest toilet block on the way.

The Kosciuszko National Park ensures proper management of the area and controls visitor impact. This is vitally important, as the area is busy during both the summer and winter because there are easy transport links from the capital, Canberra. Litter and trail erosion are minor concerns but bush and forest fires are a serious threat. Some of these are started by visitors. Campfires are prohibited above 1,700 metres – only fuel stoves are allowed in the hope that this reduces fire accidents.

My intention was to run the route, like a fell-run in the Lake District, to keep myself fit, but even the best-laid plans can go to waste. Arriving in Cooma on the bus from Canberra, I was dismayed to learn that transport was not operating further on because it was out of season. It was the summer holidays, which felt somewhat strange, having just celebrated Christmas back in England. Having no driving licence, I was faced with the prospect of expensive taxis to take me further. With the threat of bush fires in the forty-degree heat, the park was closed to visitors. Dismayed, walking out of the tourist office, I considered my options. On the bus, I had been chatting to a mother and son on their way for a vacation in a lodge in Perisher. Seeing me outside looking decidedly downcast, she asked me what the problem was. I told her about my predicament. Andrew, who had come to pick them up, invited me to stay with them for a few days. I could have bitten off his hand. The dangers of hitch hiking never occurred to me. Here I was at the age of forty, hitchhiking for the first time in my life. I took up his generous offer and slept on the floor in their games room for three nights. I met three generations of their family. Andrew's mother was fascinated by my tales of adventure. She, in turn, told me about her holidays in the foothills of the Himalaya.

I could see this region was geared up for the skiing season but the presence of snow-manufacturing companies indicated that global warming was having a huge impact. Artificial snow was an expensive option and the Australian Government could not keep on subsidising the skiing industry. Visitors could just book cheap flights to their neighbour New Zealand where there are better skiing opportunities.

In return for accommodation, Andrew and Jason, his son-in-law, wanted to go up to Kosciuszko. My plans of running it were squashed but it was a small price to pay for travelling all this way to bag the summit. We went via the Charlotte's Pass route, avoiding the more congested Thredbo area. We set off before dawn at around 5.45 a.m. Thankfully, since we had arrived, the soaring temperatures had cooled and the park had reopened. I set off with just a small rucksack, knowing that we would be back by midday. Looking at Andrew's 100-plus-litre bag I thought, 'What on earth has he got in there?' It is good to be prepared but that was over the top. Climbers who pack for every scenario usually end up doubling up on what is actually required.

I have always liked being up before dawn, apart from the chattering of birds, there is a calmness about it. We took the Range Walk, going in a horseshoe back to the car park. Once it was light, we could see Seaman's Hut on the other side. The horseshoe reminded me of being in the Brecon Beacons, in South Wales. As light came, the wind got up but it was nothing compared to Camp 3 on Everest. This wind had a warmth about it and it was pleasant, not bitingly cold, as I had experienced during my previous trips; we could see for miles. The vegetation off the path was parched from the long, dry hot summer, and I was soon carrying Andrew's rucksack because the 'kitchen sink' he had brought became a burden and my pace was stronger. Just after 9 a.m. we summited Kosciuszko, a quarter of the height of Everest. We were the first ones that day, beating the hordes who would soon arrive from the chairlift at Crackenback. Six down, one to go, I thought as I posed for photographs, my mascot giraffe in my hand. The conditions were far more palatable and my giraffe was not stuck frozen to my oxygen line. This was all very civilised compared to Everest; there were gravel tracks, a new toilet block, information plaques detailing the history of the mountain and cairns built at the summit. Coming down, we came the way of Rawson's Pass, passing the well-built Seaman's Hut. It was equipped very much like a refuge hut in the Alps. Crossing the Snowy River, we were back at the car park just after midday. Thanking Andrew and his family for their hospitality, I made my way to Sydney. I could relax now. The long haul to Australia was successful. Mission completed and I spent the rest of the holiday backpacking from Sydney to the Blue Mountains and then back to Melbourne. I actually enjoyed the hot weather, having experienced two previous summers of wet weather in Cornwall. People asked me why I did not go in the winter. My answer is that lugging all my climbing equipment that way for seven hours of walking seemed pointless. It's not as if I have not experienced enough snow and extreme conditions in the quest for the seven summits. I was also fairly sure there would be snow in Antarctica.

CHAPTER 12

THE WAITING GAME

I have not put any financial strain on myself
in my pursuit of the seven summits.
I will not carry the burden for many years to come.

— ED BUCKINGHAM

I had been advised to pay my deposit for Antarctica nine months in advance, so not long after I arrived home I booked my next trip. I expected the expedition to take three weeks, but allowing days lost through bad weather, it could have taken anything up to five weeks. Unlike Everest, where I had the uncertainty of going higher than I ever had before, I envisaged this trip to be very similar to Denali, except I was ascending to an altitude of 4,897 metres. The interior of Antarctica is a vast expanse of real wilderness. It is a high, cold plateau, with very little precipitation.

Vinson Massif, better known as Mount Vinson, is situated at a latitude of seventy-eight degrees south, in the southern half of the Sentinel Range and 1,200 kilometres from the South Pole. The Sentinel Range is home to the continent's six highest summits, which are primarily a collection of slender jagged peaks with narrow arêtes and steep rocky faces up to 2,500 metres in height. Vinson is less attractive to the would-be technical climber, being bulky, with eight peaks rising a short distance from the ninety-square-kilometre summit plateau. The peak was named after Carl Vinson, from Georgia, USA. Once chairman of the House Armed Services Committee, from 1935 to 1961, he put considerable pressure on the US Government to support Antarctic exploration. In November 1935, American Lincoln Ellsworth, together with pilot Hubert Hollick-Kenyon, made the first transcontinental flight over Antarctica. Setting out from Dundee Island, they were forced to land just short of the Bay of Whales when they ran out of fuel. Walking the last fifteen miles, Ellsworth caught sight of a jagged 'solitary little range', which he christened the Sentinel Range, but due to a thick bank of cloud, he was unaware there were higher summits underneath. It was not until 1957 that US Navy pilots discovered Vinson Massif. From 1958 and 1961, they determined the heights of the major peaks in the Ellsworth Mountains.

Vinson is best climbed during the summer months, from November through to January, when there is twenty-four-hour daylight, as I had experienced on Denali. I did not have to worry about my head torch battery wearing down as it had on Everest. Unlike many of the world's great mountains, the Sentinel Range generally experiences stable weather and mild, low temperatures. However, low atmospheric pressure at the Poles produces cold winds that rush outwards at high speeds and being caught in high winds on the summit plateau of Vinson is best avoided. Temperatures can fall to minus thirty-five degrees on a calm day and frostbite is an ever-present threat. On the flip side, the constant daylight and the hole in the ozone layer can cause sunburn

In 1966/1967, an American Antarctic mountaineering expedition was the first major project launched with the objective of climbing Mount Vinson. The US Government was keen to launch it, as rumours spread of what Woodrow Wilson Sayre was about to attempt. A somewhat eccentric American, Sayre had already blotted his copybook with a clandestine attempt on Everest from Tibet, in 1962. The government, unhappy about

Sayre's logistical organisation, feared it would have to be forced into instigating a huge and costly rescue operation. Early in December 1966, a ski-equipped US Navy Hercules landed eleven first-rate American mountaineers on the Nimitz Glacier. This was a little over eighteen miles from the summit of Vinson Massif. After establishing the three camps, Barry Corbet, John Evans, Bill Long and Pete Schoening reached the highest point in Antarctica on 17 December. Later in the month, two other ascents were made by other members of the team. The expedition stayed forty days during which time six peaks were climbed including the four highest in the range. Tyree, the second highest (at only forty-five metres lower) proved to be the most challenging prize for Corbet and Evans. They remain the only partnership to have climbed all three highest peaks in Antarctica.

In 1979, Antarctica was finally climbed for the fourth time when a largely American scientific expedition resurveyed the Ellsworth Mountains. A few days before Christmas, two Germans, Buggisch and Von Gizycki, were joined by a Soviet surveyor, Samsonov. They made an unauthorised ascent and left a red pennant on the summit. Though the ascent was frowned upon by the authorities, it allowed the scientists on the ice cap to make a much more accurate height measurement of the summit. By using satellite Doppler techniques, they arrived at the altitude recorded today. The third successful expedition, making the fifth and sixth ascents in 1983, included Dick Bass, on his way to collecting the seven summits.

In January 1991, the late Austrian mountaineer Rudi Lang soloed the mountain by way of a new route. He climbed directly from the Branscomb Glacier up the hanging glacier on the West Face. The following year, American Robert Anderson soloed two new routes. One was the South Face (Sunshine Wall) and the other was the West-South-West, or Rolex, Ridge. Since then, several routes have been added to the South and West

Faces including the Slovenian route which was climbed very quickly by Viki Groselj and his party.

There are two routes, the Normal Route via the Branscomb Glacier and the Slovenian Route. The Normal Route is similar to the West Buttress of Denali, being a long glacier expedition with no technical difficulties. From Base Camp, the route climbs gently up the Branscomb Glacier for three miles to the base of the icefall. This leads to the col between Vinson and Shinn. From the top camp, placed above the icefall, the route heads south up low-angled slopes of bare wind-scoured ice to a short, steep snow and ice face leading to the summit ridge. Generally the ascent takes six to ten days. This is the route I took. The Slovenian Route is climbed in a single push. First climbed by Viki Groselj's group, it takes a steep ice couloir from halfway up the Branscomb Glacier to the summit plateau.

The only practical way for most mountaineers to get to Vinson is by means of Adventure Network International (ANI). Following the seventh ascent of Vinson, in November 1985, ANI was set up. Three members of that summit party, Giles Kershaw from the UK, and Canadians Pat Morrow and Martyn Williams, founded the organisation. Kershaw had worked previously for British Antarctic Survey prior to the Transglobe and Footsteps for Scott expeditions. He had been the adventurous pilot who flew in the 1983 Antarctica expedition and was rapidly gaining great respect as probably the most experienced of polar aviators. The three men recognised there was a potential market for a commercial organisation that could supply the necessary logistical support for an increasing number of mountaineers wanting to stand on top of Antarctica's highest peak. Tragically in March 1990, Kershaw was killed in a gyrocopter crash on the peninsula while involved in a filming project. Subsequently the running of the company was taken on by his widow, Anne. Operations were expanded to meet the growing demand by mountaineers and virtually all ascents by Vinson, to date, have been made via the infrastructure of ANI. The company's policy is to review climbers before accepting them for a guided ascent. In 2013, a return trip to Vinson Massif for around twelve to fourteen days, cost just short of 40,000 American dollars.

In 1987, the company created the Patriot Hills blue-ice runway and tented camp at eighty degrees south. Clients are flown from Punta Arenas, Chile, in a Hercules, offering an exciting landing as it is impossible to apply brakes on the ice runway. Patriot Hills is only open for four months of the year and from there it is a one-hour flight by the ski-equipped Twin Otter to Vinson Base Camp. In 1992, this camp was moved from the Nimitz Glacier to the Branscomb to allow easier access to the Normal Route. Since ANI and the seven summits quests, the mountain has seen many ascents. The majority of climbers use guided companies because of the very high cost of operating a rescue. ANI has stringent rules for accepting independent non-guided groups, causing frustration for some, as it is a straightforward ascent. It is the remote location and extreme cold that makes it a serious undertaking and simple mistakes could have dire consequences. Recently parties have come to explore other parts of the range. The rock in the Sentinel Range is mostly metamorphic and very loose, though there are some stable areas of green quartzite. This leaves it open to the creation of technical ascents. More challenging and difficult climbs are found on the spiky succession of peaks that extend northwards along the range.

It will probably be several decades before there is a regular service to the Antarctic interior that the 'average mountaineer' can afford. However, many climbers are willing and able to pay great sums to access this remote region. With this in mind, and with the growing popularity of the seven summits challenge, Vinson is sure to have a captive audience for many years to come.

In 1959, the Antarctic Treaty was set up. No one country owns any part of the continent but several countries maintain territorial claims. There are now over fifty countries belonging to the treaty. The original treaty does not mention tourism but there are a set of guidelines that address the environmental protection of Antarctica. Hazardous goods are to be removed and the treaty bars incineration. ANI requires climbers to remove every trace, including human waste, from the continent. This policy provides excellent protection for Vinson and the Sentinel Range.

Putting Vinson aside, I settled back into life in Cornwall, work and Tamar Trotters. Soon after I had jumped off the plane from Australia, I joined a group of Trotters on a Tough Guy event in late January. From forty-degree heat, I went into freezing conditions, wading through ice and trudging through sticky mud on an assault course. I had an enjoyable weekend though I think for some it was an eye opener. It rounded off a very good January for me after Christmas, when it is traditionally busy working for Royal Mail. My Antarctica trip was booked for the same time of year. One thing I have learnt from mountaineering is patience, not only on trips but also the weeks and months leading up to them. Looking back over my seven summits challenge, I can appreciate how some people bounce off one and almost immediately attempt another. Following Everest, I could have done Koscuiszko and then prepared for Vinson that winter. But I was restricted by the financial burden and the need to take several weeks' annual leave. Everest and Vinson were by far the most expensive. I did not want to leave myself with huge crippling debts for the rest of my life. I also have a mortgage and bills to pay. I did consider selling my house but mountaineering, realistically, will only last for so long. I still have to live somewhere.

Looking back, I did not have the experience or stamina when I climbed Aconcagua, at twenty-eight, that I have now. I am not sure I could have bounced off that one and gone and done Vinson within a couple of months.

People talk about 'piling on the calories'. I think that is more easily done in the mother country rather than somewhere where the food and culture are very different.

My talks were still popular and after my trip to Antarctica, I received requests to return and talk about the seven summits. 'Hang on a minute, let me go and do it first,' I thought, but they were right. Part of the enjoyment for me is talking about my adventures and I have never had a bad response from a talk yet, so I keep going for the expectant fans. In the back of my mind, I was putting together a book of my fifteen-year adventure and the talks were bringing back the memories for me. As Vinson would be a big trip, I again wanted to raise money for the British Heart Foundation and hopefully get some recognition on television. I also wanted to advertise Tamar Trotters as even though I had only been part of it a short while, I was enjoying it immensely. I had to watch myself, as there is so much to do – marathons, ultras, half marathons, off-road events. There was an explosion of interest in the triathlon events, following the success of the Brownlee brothers in the 2012 Olympics.

My vision was that if I was successful in my quest for the seven summits, I could be a mentor at the club for any would-be members, offering advice, training, equipment and recommend companies. I wondered if I could garner the same level of interest as the triathlons. I ended up doing an extended talk one evening for the Trotters on a stage at the rugby club. I was aware how boisterous some of the Trotters get when consuming alcohol and was concerned this might spoil the talk for others. I decided to show more pictures to extend the talk but not allow for a break. I also put rows of chairs just down from the stage, pulling people away from the bar.

The evening was a success, attracting about sixty people. I raised about 400 pounds for British Heart Foundation and earned some rave reviews on Facebook. As I talked, I looked around the clubhouse. Even the most hardened drinkers of the club were transfixed, taken in by what I was talking about. I have never seen drinks neglected for so long. I thought the alcohol had evaporated rather than having been consumed. I talked for about one hour and twenty minutes and I could have heard a pin drop. What I did learn was that Trotters are not ones for theatre, they dictated when they felt it was time to stop talking and take their seats for the performance. I somehow do not think it would be approved of in the Theatre Royal but it did make me chuckle. They are always on the lookout for new members and it would be great if I could encourage more people to join. My talk also created a couple of opportunities for me, like attending the A level awards at my old comprehensive school, as a past pupil and inspiration. It is both an honour and a challenge to be asked to speak in front of proud parents. I applaud initiative shown by others, especially youngsters. Freya Phelps, aged ten, championed my cause by asking her teachers if I could visit her primary school to deliver a talk.

One of the questions I get is, 'What new challenge are you going to do after the seven summits?' My answer is that I will talk and write about it. I honestly couldn't say what I would do until I had executed the final chapter. I hoped that I would be relieved and contented but I can see by people's reactions that they do not believe it. 'Joe Public' perceives that I have a wonderful life travelling to all these wild, adventurous places. I do, don't get me wrong, but it is the sacrifices I make at home to make these trips happen. I miss socialising, going out for meals and having a few drinks. I do not see myself scaling the other twelve 8,000-metre peaks. I have no doubt in my mind that I could attempt and possibly conquer a few more but besides the cost, there is a risk involved. Switching off for that split second could cost me my life. I relate it to driving; the more a person drives, the more opportunity they have to be involved in an accident. Do I need to put myself through high altitude, extreme weather conditions, avalanches, fatigue, injury and dehydration again when I have climbed the highest mountain in the world?

I went to Antarctica having just turned forty-one, entering my fifteenth year of mountaineering and feeling far fitter than I ever had. But the strength comes from the mind. If the mind is not positive, then it is an uphill battle and in mountaineering that can prove fatal. At the present time I see myself as somebody coming out of the navy. Pete Walmsley of Trotters came out at forty, two weeks older than me. He's a very good runner, at a level I could only dream about. Though we have led very different lifestyles and careers, I feel as though I have achieved something of which to be proud. The lack of recognition for my achievements bugged me for a while after Everest but sometimes it requires others to put forward the name of an unsung hero. Through my talks, adulation finally came my way early in September 2013. I was nominated by the Bards of the Cornish Gorsedh in the Exceptional Endeavour Award category for an outstanding Cornish achievement meriting international recognition. In English and the Cornish language, it meant:

The First Cornishman to conquer Everest and raise a banner Kernewek on the Summit. An kynsa Kernow dhe fetha Everest ha sevel a baner Kernewek war an gwarthau.

Standing in a line of other category nominees, with an audience circled around us, I waited for my name to be called. The weather in Cornwall is unpredictable but the showers were holding off, very apt for the ceremony, I thought. As my name was called, I stepped forward to a huge cheer of congratulations and appreciation of my achievement. I received my award from Barbara Shaw, menternor a'n Ertach, upholder of the Heritage. Saying a few words, Barbara explained that she came from Saltash and that it gave her great personal pleasure to present the award. It was a proud moment for me and my family. My brother came down from Kent, which was a surprise to me. It was my version of the BAFTAs, which left me wondering whether I could follow up with another award in 2014.

Along with a personal certificate, I received a trophy with my name on a little shield at the base. I joined an elite band of Cornish men and women who have done great things for the county. Some of the names included Pete Goss, the yachtsman; Julie Kitchen, fourteen times Muay Thai boxing champion and Tassy Swallow, a young Cornish surfer who carried the Olympic flag. I received this award, presented by the Grand Bard, at the Gorsedh Ceremony in Penryn, Cornwall, at the site of the circle in Glasney Field on College Hill.

Cornwall is often overlooked when funding is distributed from Westminster. Many Cornish towns rely on good weather in the summer months to help survive through the winter. Certainly the summers of 2011 and 2012 did not help their causes as the weather was atrocious, turning visitors and holidaymakers away. The availability of cheap chain hotels has killed many bed and breakfasts and hotel accommodation within Cornwall. Westminster turned a blind eye to that and instead increased the landing charges at Heathrow and Gatwick from Newquay further severing the south-west from the capital. Newquay airport is fighting to stay open and its neighbouring airport, Plymouth, has already closed. Plymouth claims to be a big city but it has no airport. Many business people have to travel on Sundays because there is no rail or air link to accommodate them for Monday morning appointments in the capital. In our so-called modern world, is it good for relationships or for young families to have their weekends cut short?

Once the summer of 2013 heated up, after a cold spring, I found myself becoming leaner and fitter through running with the Trotters on club nights and competing in various races at the weekend. My trip to Antarctica was always at the back of my mind. I would need to bulk up to help withstand the severe cold I would experience. I knew there was no way I would replace the calories I burned with the limited supply of food I would consume on the trip. With that in mind, I went for a health check one morning. Having been to these workshops before, I knew what to expect. The only thing that appeared to have changed was that the equipment was all linked up to a computer, as is the norm these days. My weight, pulse, body mass index, blood pressure and a host of other scientific things were measured. As I waited for the results, the machine duly produced a till receipt, just like the ones you receive at the supermarket. Together with a handbook to accompany the receipt, I was dispatched, having been told my health was fine and that I had no worries. Studying the manual and receipt at home, I was, as I suspected, fitter than I had ever been, though I was heavier than I was at my last checkup, but it would have been unrealistic to ascertain that everything was positive. When I think about it, I find it quite staggering. I have climbed two 8,000-metre peaks and I am now fitter, at forty-one, than I was before attempting either of them. Two months prior to Antarctica, I adjusted my training. My plan was to ease back on the running and supplement it with bulk training with a rucksack. More importantly, I ate more to regain some of the 'muffin top' I had spent years trying to lose.

CHAPTER 13

MY SWANSONG

*The last three mountains you have been coming
down here and saying this will be your last.*

— DR WEBSTER HARRISON

The team trying to conquer Vinson comprised Chris, Mark, François, Nick and myself. If Chris, François and I were successful, Vinson would be the finale of our seven summits dream. Mark and Nick still had one more continent to conquer. Mark, a New Zealander, had taken ten months off work for mountaineering. He was leaving the South Col of Everest until last, hoping to have completed the challenge by early summer 2014. Upon meeting the other team members, I was struck by how experienced we all were. We had all climbed Cho Oyu, Denali and Aconcagua and François had climbed many more mountains. He had visible scars as a daily reminder. François was in his mid-fifties and came from Alsace, France. His portfolio included four 8,000-metre peaks. He was part of a climbing party on Everest the year I succeeded. On another expedition, while climbing Shishapangma (8,027 metres) with a French mate, he got caught in an avalanche which left him with concussion and having lost a mitten. His mate left him to survive the night alone. The next morning, another French climber came across François and seeing that he was clearly in some distress, got him down safely but at some cost: François suffered frostbite to some fingers and toes, which resulted in amputation, leaving him with a claw-like left hand. Strangely enough François never heard from his mate again. After all that, François was still determined to return to the mountains.

We met in the new building in Punta Arenas in Chile, which housed Adventure Network International. It had been a long flight for me from Heathrow, but Chile was not the final destination. We still had to fly to Antarctica. After an early morning wake-up call and kit check, I went off to get my briefing, which was delivered by Mike Sharp, one of the co-owners. He explained the logistics of getting to Union Glacier Camp and informed us about the Antarctic Treaty and the preservation of Antarctica. He ended by saying that there was a good chance we would be flying out that night as the weather was fine.

Sure enough, that evening I left the luxurious Dreams Hotel and went to the airport. I had been in Punta Arenas less than twenty-four hours. I was feeling jet lagged but we were buying ourselves time on the mountain in the event of bad weather. This was, after all, a once-in-a-lifetime experience. Catching up on sleep was a minor detail. The Ilyushin flight was something to which I was particularly looking forward. It was a big Russian Hercules-type jet holding eighty-four tonnes of fuel and carrying seventeen tonnes of cargo. A return journey to Antarctica used seventy tonnes with the rest in reserve. The back came down where the cargo was loaded and it was tied down with big rope nets. Passengers were seated to the front. The flight took around four-and-a-half hours but because we were heading south, the time zone was the same. After clearing security at the airport, I walked out on to the runway to board the plane. It was huge and with its torso bulging, it looked overweight and squat to the ground. Its wings looked like short stubby arms.

Walking round the front, I noticed the nose was rounded and squashed in the centre. Before boarding the plane, I had to walk through a tray of pink substance. It was a biosecurity measure to ensure we didn't transport soil or seeds into Antarctica. Entering the plane, I could see right through, with daylight piercing from the rear. Above, there were huge winches and pulleys on rails designed to transfer loads weighing up to seventeen tonnes. There were no windows but a huge screen had been erected so we were able to watch the flight. With the rear ramp down for loading and the passenger door open, the cold engulfed the plane. Once we were seated, the Russian captain gave a briefing and the plane prepared to take off. The noise of the engines was a cacophony that turned into a roar; I was thankful of my ear plugs. Once we were cocooned in the plane, it soon warmed up. The flight was quite entertaining as I watched the guides come round with water, sweets, crisps, sandwiches and chocolate. They did a good job but they did not quite have the glamour of most airline hostesses. After being fed, I became very weary and fell asleep, content on a full stomach. Waking from my nap, I noticed the screen had been turned off to avoid any panic as we descended on to the Union Glacier in Antarctica. I imagine it was quite unnerving for those with a delicate stomach. The landing on to the Union Glacier is tricky. Specially designed, the ice runway is very long to allow the plane to slow down naturally as it is not possible to apply brakes on ice. Our landing was very smooth but it did take a while for the plane to grind to a halt. To slow and eventually stop something of the Ilyushin's size and mass must take some doing and I imagine it is extremely challenging.

Finally, I had arrived, after two and a half years of planning and saving. Taking my first steps on to the ice, I nearly slipped and I had to be helped like a frail old man. Breaking a leg or ankle stepping on to the ice would have been a great start to my final continent attempt. Walking tentatively, I looked around. The mountains seemed so far away, such was their vastness. Our isolation struck me; we had been offloaded into the middle of nowhere. It was gone 2 a.m. but it was daylight. I was wearing sunglasses to shield my eyes from the UV rays. Ushered into the vehicles, we were transported five miles to camp. The track was hard, compacted snow. All things considered the road was good, in fact, it was better than some of the potholed roads in Cornwall after two consecutive harsh winters. As I looked back, the sight of the Ilyushin shrank to a dot as we sped further away, the last link I had to civilisation. This did not concern me as I was there for the challenge and the remoteness. People can be obsessed with communication and the comfort of normal day-to-day life. My mobile phone, besides the camera, was useless. Any calls to home had to be made by a satellite phone which I had no intention of using until I came back down from Vinson.

The main Antarctic camp lies on the broad expanse of Union Glacier, in the southern Ellsworth Mountains. From there, it is a short flight to Vinson and just over 600 miles to the South Pole. Majestic peaks rose all around but we had to travel before reaching the foot of them. On arrival at camp, I was shown to the tent Mark and I would share. We slept in Clam Tents, which cost 6,000 American dollars and generally lasted five seasons. The constant UV rays fade the fabric and, over time, it wears and loses its strength. The tents were double-walled, roomy, with camp beds either side. It all seemed very civilised indeed with a table and some bowls and towels. It took me back to Kilimanjaro and the first night spent under canvas. A high-tech nylon covering was stretched over a durable aluminium frame. This design was used by Shackleton's Endurance expedition. In fact, the tents were named after expedition members and explorers like Amundsen and Charrard. Mark and I were staying in Palmer. The whole camp was laid out in a similar pattern. In a small way, it reminded us what early expeditions were like, but how could it ever really compare when so much time had passed?

Just after we had settled in at 3 a.m. we were surprised to be provided with a full cooked meal consisting of beef stew, vegetables and a tantalising dessert. The chunks of beef were so tender and succulent, they melted in the mouth. If this was anything to go by, I needn't have feared losing weight. The dining tent was the heart of the camp, complete with a kitchen at the far end. It also had an extensive library of books that had been donated by previous explorers. There we received daily weather bulletins and reports about other current expeditions. The dining tent served as a gathering place to meet others setting off on their various adventures. At nearly 5 a.m. I turned in for the night, or was it day?

After a comfortable rest on the camp bed, I woke to the news that we would be transferring to Vinson Base Camp, at 2,100 metres, later that day. It felt strange waking up the same day without a period of darkness. Eye masks were a necessity for this trip. A forty-minute flight on a Twin Otter plane took us through more of the vast range of Antarctica to the cosy Base Camp on the Branscomb Glacier. Looking down with a bird's eye view I saw nothing that really stood out to me, unlike Everest when I was flying over the Himalaya. My assumption that Antarctica would be similar to Alaska was wrong. I could see never-ending ranges under a cloudless blue sky. With no animal tracks or human footprints, it was as though we were the first visitors to descend on Antarctica. At Vinson Base Camp, we were served freshly cooked meals in a heated dining tent. Nearby, we slept in individual mountaineering tents with a toilet positioned off the runway, looking down the valley. The camp was more basic and it was quieter than at Union. I could feel our sheer remoteness from the outside world.

Once the plane took off down the runway and disappeared into the blue, we were on our own, camping in the wild. On landing, we were met by a scruffy young man with a straggly beard. He was called Josh. He originated from Anchorage, Alaska and he spoke with a slow drawl. Josh gave me the feeling that everything was very laid-back, with none of the time constraints and deadlines of normal suburbia. As long as the weather forecast was good, we were free to walk when we liked, with the advantage of twenty-four hour daylight. We learnt that back in Alaska, Josh had spent some time in the film industry. This explained his big director's chair. If it was sunny, he would place his chair outside at the top of the camp and look down at the picturesque valley. The chair gave the impression of real authority. He learnt that he would shortly be handing over the role of Base Camp manager to come and join us on the climb up the mountain. Over dinner, we met our other leader, Robert Smith, an experienced guide who was born in Ireland and lived in Scotland. No wonder he had spent a few years on the sunnier and drier continent of Antarctica, escaping all the rain and gloom.

The next morning, it was time to get out all the equipment that we would be using and make any modifications on recommendation from Rob and Josh. It is not uncommon for leaders to want to check the kit. They want to know what hardware each climber has and advise on what works best on a particular mountain, things like putting idiot loops on gloves and a layer of padding around the top of a steel ice-axe as insulation from the cold. We also attached pack leashes and sledge loops to the rucksacks to prepare for the day when we would pull up to Low Camp. After a productive morning, we went out on an acclimatisation walk in readiness for the height of Low Camp. This was a chance for the guides to assess our fitness. Chris, from Alaska, was an accomplished skier. Living with Denali on his doorstep, he had used it as his playground, climbing it twice, once on skis and once during an adventure in his snow mobile. Chris had a voice that carried and he never had a problem conveying his meaning or capturing an audience. Though we could not always see him, we could always hear him. He was a likeable chap, regaling us with his stories of illegally being on Denali in his snow machine, getting up Motorcycle Hill and dodging the national park authorities. He reminded me of Ben on Kilimanjaro because he never harboured any fear of the possible consequences and he displayed great bravado. Up to Low Camp, he was paired with Rob on skis. During the day's afternoon walk, we aimed to gain the same height as Low Camp, at around 2,880 metres. Nick and Mark were on Josh's rope team, while François and I went with Namgya. Namgya was a guide from Nepal who was coming back from an anterior cruciate ligament injury that needed constructing in Punta Arenas. It was caused while he was learning to ski the previous year. The first part of the hill was now called Nangya Hill. Here were two people who seriously had something in common and could share stories of the long road back from injury. This was the first real exercise I had done after all my travelling and I found I was lethargic to start with. Most of the way, we travelled in powdery snow but as we climbed up to the left of the hill, the ground became harder underfoot. Down in the valley, we could see some groups pulling sledges en route to Low Camp, making a cache and returning to Base Camp. From a distance, it looked like a plane leaving a vapour trail in the sky.

We were getting used to the clothing and layering. It was important to be comfortable and not to have too many layers on because if we sweated buckets, we would have cooled down quicker and, in extreme cases, developed hypothermia. On reaching our summit, we paused and looked around. The range reminded me of the Himalaya with its mixture of peaks of all sizes but they stretched further into the distance. In total, the journey took us around five hours, about the same time it would take to get to Low Camp. I was pleased to get some exercise and stretch the stiffness out of my plane legs. This was the first exercise I had undertaken since I departed from England on Boxing Day.

The next day we moved to Low Camp. This was the hardest carry of the trip but, thankfully, we had enough food cached so we only had to carry a small amount, together with our personal belongings. Previous trips undertaken this season had left food in Low Camp, which was a bonus. As we were a small group, we only had to move once and did not have to return again, which bought us time in case the unpredictable weather prevented us from making progress on the mountain. We ascended 650 metres over a gradually rising glacier with some crevassing. Opposite to Denali, I decided to experiment with distributing the weight between my sledge and rucksack. I wanted to see if it was more tiring pulling from the hips as opposed to carrying the weight on my back. Comparison was hard though as this was our only day of load carrying. This time we were spared the experience of Denali where we spent several days bearing heavy loads at high altitude. The snow conditions were also different. On Denali there was more snow and if we had to break trail, it was hard work. With no significant snowfall on Vinson, travelling was a lot easier.

Many of the routes are reasonably hard with compacted snow and ice built up over time, making it firm. It was quite idyllic really because we were not sweating and dehydrating so much under the low sun. The route was made easier by the weather, as it was cloudy which kept the sun off and the temperature down. I had confidence in my colleagues that if I went through the ice, they would be quick to react and prevent me plunging deep in the crevasse. Although we were not walking side by side, teamwork was vital. We were still roped up and travelling at equal lengths apart, maintaining discipline in our movement and speed. Like on Denali, sometimes we were crossing crevasses so keeping the rope tight was imperative. Peeing en route was a vastly different experience to Denali. We did not pee on site, we either used a pee bottle or one of the designated pee holes. This was another example of waste management on the mountain. I thought Denali was clean but Antarctica raised the bar. It is, however, easier to keep something clean when there are only around two hundred visitors, as opposed to around twelve hundred.

With a few rest breaks, we hauled into Low Camp after around five hours. Low Camp was nestled at the foot of the high mountain not far from the ascent up the fixed ropes. A big tent, used as a kitchen, was already set up but we had to help put up tents among the fortified ice-block walls. The air felt colder and I experienced the discomfort of the unpleasant contact of the aluminium tent pegs and poles on my bare fingers. This is where I learnt to work with gloves on, trying to keep in the warmth. I kept moving and working to keep warm and not let my fingers get too cold, which was not easy to do when I was fiddling with tents and banging in stakes. It was New Year's Eve and the majority of alcohol was down at Vinson Base Camp. As Rob and the fellow guides radioed through with updates, I could tell Patchy and her crew were getting more merry and jovial as midnight came nearer. Patchy was the new Base Camp manager, relieving Josh of his duties so he could play on the mountain. We had managed to haul up two litres of red wine but evenly distributed between nine, it did not amount to much. We had gone round the other tents at Low Camp and invited them to the massive tent for our wild party, privately hoping they would decline our offer to share our meagre rations. Fortunately, only two took up the offer, Jo from Mountain Trip and Geradth from Alpine Ascents. It could have been a lot worse. Jo was from Alaska and immediately created a rapport with Chris. As a neighbouring guide, he already knew Josh. Geradth was from Oregon and had spent time working in the offices of Alpine Ascents before having a crack at guiding on mountains. With the New Year in, we went to bed to sober up before the morning.

Even though there was twenty-four hour daylight, from about 3 a.m. the temperature dropped dramatically. Climbing in the shade greatly increased our chances of developing frostbite and other cold-related problems so it was important to pack an extra fleece and an extra pair of gloves. New Year's Day was predominantly a rest day. We woke up to the smell of pancakes and then practised rope movements on the fixed lines. Josh and Rob set up a mock rope area where we practised using ascenders and karabiners. Though we were experienced climbers, the activity was a useful refresher and helped me get used to wearing mitts. It allowed Josh and Rob to evaluate our technical skills. The fixed-rope section was the trickiest stretch of the whole climb. Unlike Josh and Rob, the rest of us had no need to use karabiners and ascenders in our daily working lives so familiarising ourselves with the equipment could not be a bad thing.

Later that afternoon, we did a two-hour walk, passing the fixed lines en route. I thought it looked difficult and I was daunted by the steep gradient but I felt sure that once I was on it, it would be no more difficult than steep sections on other mountains. This was the hardest day and I was grateful that we were only ascending once and we didn't have to make a cache. The ascent was 1,020 metres. It took us six to eight hours to navigate a 1,200-metre fixed rope section, of up to forty-five-degree angles, with rocky sections of blue ice. We were strongly advised to take our time. Chris left his skis at Low Camp to join a rope group. I was paired with Nick, with Rob guiding. Privately, I was not impressed because I felt that Nick would slow me down. Even though we were the same age, I felt my fitness level was stronger. He had already shown signs of finding the walks difficult. So far, I had just been going through the motions, catching up on sleep after my flights and adapting to the time zone difference. My stamina and strength tends to increase as a holiday goes on; I don't use it all up at the start. I would have to prove myself because once I was on the fixed ropes, I was on my own. We were expected to govern our own speed. If we came up behind traffic, we had to use our nouse and only pass where it was safe to do so, like at the pitons.

The next day, it was time to move up. The weather report at noon said gusts of twenty-five to thirty miles per hour winds were to be expected up high. The temperature was still average for the time of year, around minus twenty-five degrees. Looking out of the tent, Rob and Josh decided to give it a go, warning us to be prepared to turn back if the winds were too strong. I was up for it now, having shaken off my lethargy. I wanted to prove a point. The ropes would not be busy, as we were the only group pushing for the top camp. Once on the fixed lines, I moved quickly and efficiently. The slope was not steeper or higher than the sections on Cho Oyu and Denali but it was longer. Champing at the bit, I made the ground up between me and Chris, who was the last member of his rope team. I tucked in behind him all the way to the top. The snow was mostly compact on the fixed lines and I cannot remember any areas of blue ice. In Antarctica, there is very little snowfall, which made our journey easier because we did not have to contend with piles of loose, fresh snow. I did not have to stab at the ground a couple of times just to get a satisfactory foothold. It only took me three and a half hours to get to the top of the fixed lines. I was pleased my months of training were starting to pay off.

On the fixed lines, we were sheltered from the wind but on reaching the top of the fixed ropes, we felt a change in the weather, the air was noticeably cooler so I put an extra layer on before I lost too much heat. We had a good view of Mount Shinn which, if all went well on Vinson, we would get to climb. Back on a group rope, we walked the rest of the way into camp, at 3,700 metres. There was no wind at all, at least not the gale the forecast predicted. If we had listened to the forecast, we would have wasted an opportunity. If we could bank extra days, it wouldn't be a bad thing. We set about putting up tents. Other groups had made caches but they were down at Low Camp. Unlike on Denali, there are no scavenging rooks so many caches were visible, just buried in rocks so they did not blow away. I found that digging for snow and banging in tent stakes was harder than on Denali as, with no loose rocks around, I had to use my ice-axe. I also had to dig for snow to boil water. Shovels alone bounced on top of the ice or broke, such is their brittleness. Looking up, I could clearly see the compacted pathway to the summit, up to where it rounded a corner out of sight.

Rob came up to me and said I looked strong. I agreed that I felt good and explained that I had experienced this altitude, and beyond, many times before. I felt I still had a lot more to give. On previous trips, I drank a lot more fluid to cope with the altitude but I was feeling good with no altitude-related problems. We soon realised that there was disparity between the walking speeds of the members in each rope team. François felt he was being pushed by Chris and Mark. He liked to stop and take pictures which took him longer than most with his damaged hands, so we swapped groups.

We rested the following day as other teams joined us from Low Camp, including International Mountain Guides, Alpine Ascents, the three-man Norwegian team and, later, Mountain Trip. We were now on porridge and dehydrated meals, which took double the amount of time to cook because of the altitude. Most of the food was well past its use-by date. Much to our amusement, somebody found some three-year-old salmon. A nightmare for Waitrose, but what did use-by dates matter in this great outdoor freezer?

The next day, we planned to go to the summit but the weather report was not brilliant. As the season draws on, it steadily became colder and climbers can face harsh winds on the long exposed ridge to the summit. The ascent was 1,120 metres, which would take us nine to twelve hours, a gradually rising valley with forty-degree slopes and a rocky ridge on the summit pyramid. The forecast predicted winds of twenty-five to thirty-five miles per hour, which is excessive but there was no significant low pressure. I think all weather forecasts need to be treated as a guide, not gospel. However, we went to bed early with our summit push very much hanging in the balance.

The next morning, the guides did not wake us, which gave me a clear indication that we would not be going. I was disappointed. Lying in my tent, I listened for the wind. I could not feel the tents blowing furiously. Not rushing to get out of my sleeping bag, I also listened to what was going on around camp. I heard Chris get up, he was clearly of the opinion the weather was good enough to go. I got the distinct impression that if he made plans to go out in Alaska, he went whatever the weather. I could not envisage Chris sitting around for days on end. There had already been a few days on this trip where we hadn't made any progress. He proceeded to have a heated exchange with Rob with the upshot being that the weather would be assessed again after breakfast. The confrontation had clearly worked because over breakfast Rob and Josh changed their minds – we were back on. It was true, it appeared fine down at High Camp but ahead of us lay uncertainty. I think anybody making a summit attempt should have in mind that they may have to turn back.

Why do tragedies occur? Poor snow conditions, exposed slopes, changing weather and high altitude are just some of the reasons. This was exactly what we faced on Vinson, besides the snow conditions which are the same virtually all season. Summit fever was striking me again but with the added bonus of Vinson being the finale to my seven summits quest. The two-and-a-half years of waiting since my Everest expedition had come down to the next ten hours. I tried to keep in mind that we still had plenty of time to make the climb. Roping up, I was now on Josh's rope and I purposely placed myself behind him. Even though I was not setting the pace, I wanted Josh to feel no tension on the rope. I would make sure there was just enough slack so Josh was not pulling me up, but knew I was behind him step by step.

We left camp and traversed up a gradually inclining valley, the weather was calm and we got into a steady rhythm. Like on any mountain, we tended to walk for an hour before stopping for a maximum of ten minutes, before our bodies cooled down excessively. It was just enough time to have a drink or a bite to eat. After a couple of hours of climbing, the weather conditions and the conditions underfoot had changed, it was now windier and we were walking on more blue ice. This was a new experience for me. It felt like I was walking on broken glass. I felt I should dance across it quickly but the best way to negotiate blue ice is to plant the feet firmly and stomp across, definitely and purposely. Nevertheless, I was feeling fine. Energy was pumping though my body so fast I could feel it. My torso and my feet were warm and I wore my mitts to save my fingers from possible frostbite. As the ridge to the summit is long and exposed and does not provide shelter from the wind, we took an alternative route off to the right and traversed up a col to reach the ridge just before the final summit pyramid. Though it was a more difficult route, there was more snow (as opposed to bare rock) so we could wear our crampons. Zigzagging our way up the col, our footwork had to be good. I had my ice-axe and rope in my uphill hand and as many of my twelve crampon points in the snow as possible. My hunger and desire was still there. I breathed steadily, slowly going up the col. I looked up to where I imagined the ridge line to be but it was always a bit further on.

Finally, we made it on to the ridge, pausing for breath before the final summit pyramid. It was a steady incline but nothing I have not experienced before. Like on Everest, I had everything in my pockets for the summit and I had no intention of taking off my rucksack. During the final walk I was smiling, privately congratulating myself. That was the extent of my emotion, no tears, but I was chuffed with my achievement. I felt like a short person desperately scrambling up over a large pommel horse. Josh was already on top, pulling in the rope for me. In turn, I did the same for Mark and he for Chris. Quickly gathering my thoughts, I became aware of the gusts of wind that struck every now and then. It was minus thirty-two with a twenty-five mile an hour wind. This was colder than Everest. A climber would not be on top of Everest in these winds but consider the height, 4,892 metres as opposed to 8,848 metres. The decreased barometric pressure at Vinson's far southern latitude means the summit feels more like 5,500 metres – that is a lot of difference. I set about taking my photos. Somebody captured a great snap of me with my St Piran's flag, in my Tamar Trotters polo shirt, holding up seven fingers, against the backdrop of the surrounding landscape stretching out for miles. I didn't really care if my St Piran's or my polo shirt was curled up. The photo captured what it was like up there in that moment. It would have been selfish of me to have asked somebody to hold my flag for me. They had their own memories to capture.

I wanted to take a photo of my two nieces out of my pocket but I could feel my hands becoming colder. It was 4 January, Jessica's third birthday. Her Uncle Ed was completing the seven summits challenge on her birthday, the first Cornishman to do so. My memories of this day and the day I summited Everest (21 May 2011) are two of my favourites. The whole seven summit challenge threw up many memorable moments. Not moments I always appreciated at the time but moments I truly treasured when looking back. François's appearance on the summit, not far behind me, reminded me again of the danger of letting body parts get too cold. He was thankful to be alive but he was living with a daily reminder of how lucky he had been to survive. Mountaineering is my hobby, not my career and I very much hope to remain working for Royal Mail for a few more years yet.

We only had ten minutes on the summit. Turning round in reverse order, we made our way slowly down, passing the other rope team and giving them gentle encouragement. The walk back down was uneventful but we took extra care not to let the rope go slack or to lose our footing. Back at

High Camp, the other teams congratulated us. They all went up the next day, in better conditions, while we rested. The guides commented on how quick we were – it had been a seven-hour round trip. Rob also told to me, privately, that he thought the climb looked easy for me. I could not deny that he was right so I said so. It was a comfortable summit for me but definitely the coldest I had experienced. My summits of Aconcagua, Denali, Cho Oyu and Everest had been a lot harder, as had been the trips as a whole. I discussed my previous ascents with the team, over a frozen meal, brought up from the Union Glacier kitchen, and a celebratory shot of twelve-year old Glenlivet whisky – a better celebration than New Year's Eve.

On 6 January, we all climbed Mount Shinn, except Nick and Josh. It was slightly smaller than Vinson but a far tougher climb. There was a lot more blue ice to negotiate, plus a vertical rocky section and a snow hill climb. The last bit was some of the steepest I have ever climbed. My feet were positioned at three o'clock to the snow and I used the point of my ice-axe. I could feel the burn in my calves from the exertion and intensity, but the hard work was worth it. The reward of reaching the summit was breathtaking and there were no winds. We spent forty minutes resting, taking photos and having a bite to eat. It just goes to show that a perfect day cannot be predicted. The climb took us eight-and-a-half hours. I understand why Shinn is an optional extra rather than the warm-up for Vinson. Had I ascended Shinn first, it may have taken me too long to recover and jeopardised my chances of summiting Vinson – an expensive miscalculation. We maintained a 100 per cent record on Vinson that season and we were the first ones to summit both mountains.

The following day, it was time to go back down to Vinson Base Camp. We packed up and made our way down the fixed line to Low Camp. The other teams had descended the day before so we had the mountain to ourselves. At Low Camp, it was solitary and eerie. The big tent stood there alone. Attaching our sledges, we made our way down, stopping a few times for photos. Patchy and Josh welcomed us wholeheartedly and congratulated us for our successful summits. There was no time to waste. We were flying back to Union Glacier that evening, with memories of a once-in-a-lifetime experience.

Taking a much-needed shower, I found myself talking to an Australian, Geoff Wilson, who had single-handedly just hauled a pair of oversized, artificial breasts across Antarctica, to within 107 kilometres of the South Pole, to raise funds for the McGrath Foundation, a charity supporting breast cancer. Richard Parks, another man returning from a solo adventure, was also in camp. He was the fastest British man in history to reach the South Pole, in a time of twenty-nine days, nineteen hours and twenty-four minutes. In the all time list Richard was second to one other. I felt humbled and honoured to be in such company. Flying back that evening, I found it hard to take in just how short a visit it had been. I had arrived on 28 December 2013 and I was now flying out on 10 January 2014.

CHAPTER 14

MY FIFTEEN-YEAR DEGREE

*I never envisaged that when I started on Kilimanjaro
I would one day climb an 8,000m peak let alone two.
To go to Antarctica was a fairytale come true.*

— ED BUCKINGHAM

So what drives me? What inspires the hunger, desire, motivation and sheer determination of completing some of the challenges that make up the seven summits? Quite simply it all came from within. There were no fitness coaches, dietitians, promoters, television or sponsorship deals. After completing the seven summits, what do I do next? That is the question I am asked by people who assume my next big adventure is on the horizon. I think it is a time for reflection; I have come to a crossroads in my life. Ben Fogle's life is a world away from mine. His expeditions are not limited by financial constraints experienced by most people. Wouldn't it be great to wake up one morning and have no financial limitations? The biggest advertising tools he has to his advantage are television and presenting. I am not bitter or resentful but what great exposure they are. At school, I never entertained the idea of television or radio playing a part in my career but who can see into the crystal ball of life? I can see now the exposure and potential offers I could have been rewarded with. Hindsight is a wonderful thing but I have always been cautious in my approach before plunging into something.

At some time or other, I could have considered becoming a professional mountaineer but I had a relatively secure job at Royal Mail, though, during the recession, there was always a possibility that I could be made redundant. And, of course, being away from Cornwall would have been hard. If I sat down and added up how much I have spent on trips since Kilimanjaro, in 1999, it probably equates to something in the region of eighty thousand pounds, including flights, equipment and specialist insurance. Where did I find that sort of money? I resisted the temptation to sell my house and there have been no cash cows or windfalls to my knowledge. I have become extremely prudent and resourceful. Just because I am single, it does not mean I have gone out and frittered money away on expensive nights on the tiles. I have been reclusive at times but determined and driven by my ultimate goal. How could I entertain being in a relationship during some of these ventures? 'I'm taking thirteen weeks leave to try and climb Everest, costing twenty thousand pounds. Don't worry, just mind the shop until I get back, if I come back.' Besides that, what about the training and mental preparation beforehand? It is a lot of extra stress on a relationship. Everest was a war of attrition. A race to acclimatise and summit before I became too weak, fell ill, or died.

There will always be people who want to climb the world's highest peak, because there's more to being on Everest than getting hemmed in by crowds or confronted by heaps of trash. Everest has become an icon for everything that is wrong with climbing. In 1963 only six people reached the top, in the spring of 2012 more than 500 made it to the summit. At the Hillary Step on 25 May, the queues were so long that some people going up were waiting more than two hours. Fortunately the weather was good, however, if a storm had descended the death toll could have been staggering. Everest is now seen as being part of a 'bucket list' of things to do. In the last five years, there has been an increasing number of deaths on the mountain, due to greater numbers of people. Now that almost 4,000 people have reached the summit, some more than once, the feat means less than it did half a century ago.

Deaths are common on the mountain, the well-published Western climbers getting trapped high on the mountain and the not always reported Sherpa deaths. The Sherpas are teams of dedicated people who maintain and fix routes. In a season, they probably go up and down the mountain twenty to twenty-five times, carrying kit and supplies to the advanced camps. The more trips they do, the more they expose themselves to dangers like crossing through the Khumbu Icefall on the south side, known as the 'popcorn section' (huge, jumbled blocks of ice that create lots of crevasses which can 'pop' at any time and cause avalanches). Nevertheless, without the Sherpas' dedication, many expeditions would hardly get off the ground.

In an effort to break existing records and create new challenges, clients are getting younger. The youngest boy to summit Everest was a thirteen-year-old American called Jordan Romero, on 22 May 2010. Tyler Armstrong summited Aconcagua at nine years old; does that mean he will scale Everest on his tenth birthday? The Sherpas are getting younger too, and they are increasingly leading people with very little knowledge or experience. Young Sherpas carrying thirty kilos on their backs earn fewer than twenty dollars a day. Is this right? Maverick climbers frequently underestimate the mountain challenge. When their poorly made plans go wrong, to whom do they turn to for help? The Sherpas. The ill-prepared mavericks squat in other teams' camps using their oxygen, provisions and camping gas.

Russell Brice of Himalayan Experience insists that it's all about good communication: 'We can manage the numbers if all the operators talk to each other instead of competing against one another.' Russell originates from New Zealand and has been operating a successful business for many years. He has led several expeditions on Everest. Another factor is low-budget outfitters. They do not always have the staff, knowledge or proper equipment to keep their clients safe if something goes wrong. The cheaper operators often employ fewer Sherpas and those they do hire sometimes lack experience. In 2012, all of the clients who died on Everest went with low-budget, less experienced operators.

I have read many books and watched DVDs about professional explorers and climbers. Many of them did not summit on their first attempts on mountains. I succeeded on all the seven summits and on Cho Oyu the first time. Cynically, some might say I got lucky but I can assure you it was more than just luck. My well-being had always been at the forefront of my mind. Sir Ranulph Fiennes sacrificed fingers and repeatedly put his body on the line to achieve his goal, even though he has a heart condition. When he suffered an angina attack climbing the north side of Everest, in 2008, he may not have survived if it had not been for the pills in his pocket. What would have happened if I had three fingers or toes amputated? I wouldn't be able to drive lorries, I would probably have to work indoors and, ultimately, I may have lost my job. If you have stuck with this book thus far, surely you can sense my passion for the outdoors.

Another question I get asked is, 'Why climb Everest?' George Mallory's response was 'because it's there.' Other mountaineers have said, 'Why not?' For me, the answer is that I love mountains, the remoteness, the challenge, the sense of achievement and being far away from everyday suburbia and my mobile phone. I have no problem with going out for the day and not speaking to anybody, whether it be on Bodmin Moor or the coastal footpath. That is what it was like on Vinson and Shinn. We had the mountains to ourselves. After a period of recovery from Cho Oyu, the lure and challenge took hold again. My initial thought was to put it all off until later in life but it caused me sleepless nights and endless daydreaming. In the end, I had to tell my parents that I had changed my mind and I would be returning to the Himalaya. I am a believer in acting on impulse. It was the right time in my life to go. I did not want to reach sixty and say, 'I wish I had tried'.

I expect that I would find it easier to climb Aconcagua now, at the age of forty-one, than I did at twenty-eight. My brother would one day like me to accompany him on his attempt to climb Aconcagua. I have told him it is a hard, hard mountain but it is in his DNA to not give up easily. I hope he will not be put off after reading chapter 3. It would be a great honour and a privilege to stand on top of Aconcagua with him. But his situation differs from mine; he has a wife and a young family to support. I now have greater stamina than I did at twenty-eight. I am leaner and fitter. Looking at the summit photos, I look punch-drunk to the point of oblivion. But was I? I do not think so. Mental strength got me through, as it had when I climbed Elbrus, Cho Oyu and Everest. I say Elbrus because I believe if I had undertaken more acclimatisation walks prior to the summit, it would have been comfortable. Denali was my most enjoyable trip. I revelled in the physical challenge of carrying and hauling sledges at high altitude. For a long time, I thought that Vinson was similar but having experienced both, I realise that they are not. To think I went to Vinson and put on weight. Denali was the turning point, the realisation of what I could achieve. I then had to delve into the Himalaya.

There are few people in mountaineering circles quite like Brian Blessed. Like the larger-than-life characters he plays, he has quite a portfolio to his name including exploits into the adventurous world. Not a man to shirk an adventure, Brian has attempted to climb Everest three times. He reached 8,600 metres in 1993 and 7,700 metres in 1996. I can picture him peering up from Camp 3 to climbers on the Second Step, his booming voice bellowing instructions or encouragement. With his voice reverberating around the mountain, it's a wonder it did not trigger an avalanche. He has climbed both Aconcagua and Kilimanjaro successfully. He was the oldest person to reach both the geographical North Pole and the magnetic North Pole. Undertaking an expedition into the jungles of Venezuela, he survived a plane crash.

Mountaineering has not only given me mental strength, but also taught me to be patient in several ways in waiting for my next expedition, for my body to acclimatise to the altitude and for suitable climbing weather. Now I think I am more patient in everyday life. I only wish I had more patience in my running with the Tamar Trotters. Having said that, I ran a good-for-age place in the Manchester 2014 marathon, below three hours and fifteen minutes, which gave me a place in the 2015 Virgin Money London Marathon, where I finished in three hours and twenty-eight minutes. Not my best run but it was my first time at the event. I was extremely pleased to get the opportunity. The atmosphere and crowds are like no other marathon in the world. I would like to become a more disciplined runner and apply better race management. I strive to be a hard worker, like my father. He has always been there for me to offer words of encouragement or another perspective on a problem. He is a good friend as well as being my dad.

I am stubborn but I draw the line at pig-headedness. There is a difference. Stubbornness is born out of determination, while pig-headedness is failing to listen and carrying on regardless, whatever the consequences. Joe Simpson is a fabulous writer but his trips are not my cup of tea. In May 1985, Joe and Simon Yates made the first ascent of the West Face of Siula Grande, Peru. Shortly after they began their descent, Simpson slipped, fell into a crevasse and broke his leg, leaving Yates with the difficult decision to cut the rope and Simpson to fall to his almost certain death. However, Simpson lived and crawled his way back to Base Camp where he found his belongings burnt as a memorial. Their story, *Touching the Void*, as told by Simpson, was later published as a book and adapted into a film. Climbing unknown routes, alpine style, without telling local authorities, is not my style. The trip could have ended tragically but Yates and Simpson's mental strength and belief is commendable indeed.

Mountaineering is a seriously dangerous sport, even before going into the Death Zone on 8,000-metre peaks. Most high mountains are littered with accounts of mortalities or near fatalities. On the 10th and 11th of May 1996, eight climbers perished on Everest. They were caught in a blizzard while going for the summit. My belief is that we can only fret so much about danger or we might never step outside our own front doors. Take my lifestyle: I am a lorry driver who works shifts deep into the night and then I am confronted with the onslaught of rush hour traffic in the morning. I think the discipline has helped me prepare for the push on a mountain. Having completed cardiovascular training and ac-climatisation, while maintaining my health in often primitive condi-tions, all that remains is the final hurdle.

The philosophy I have adopted and found to be successful is the three P's: planning where to go and what the trip will achieve; preparing by get-ting fit and buying equipment; and, during the expedition, being patient when unforeseen circumstances mean a deviation from the itinerary. On expedition, three things that made my time more enjoyable were palatable food, a chef who could cook Western-style food and being able to maintain good health and sanitation. Base Camp on Everest is pretty basic and inhumane already without feeling under the weather.

So what have I got from this experience? My certificate when I was made a Grand Bard by the Cornish Gorsedh, and my own little shield, along-side Pete Goss and Julie Kitchen. The British Summiteers of Everest list was updated in 2013. Next to number 291 (of 360) is 'Edward Buckingham, the First Cornishman'. It is a relatively small list of summits, bearing in mind some of the climbers have summited multiple times. It gives me a tremendous amount of satisfaction to be listed alongside names such as Kenton Cool. The full list of summits is dominated by Tibetans and Nepalese who are born into the region. Their bodies are naturally adjusted to the conditions and atmosphere. Sherpas produce fewer oxygen-carrying blood cells at high altitude, rather than more, which is the norm. This means they are less likely to develop long-term illnesses so they can work more.

I looked back at my expedition photographs while researching for this book. I can assure you that none of them have been altered to exaggerate the perilous conditions I endured or the beautiful landscapes I captured. My mountaineering equipment, which I built up over the years, also brings back many fond memories, the Craghoppers jacket worn from Kilimanjaro through to Vinson and the Sigg bottle which rolled down the rocks like a weeble, is battered but not punctured. These items provide me with many stories I can share with audiences.

My public speaking has resurfaced. I now offer Everest, Antarctica and seven summits presentations. The response from audiences has been brilliant and word of mouth has generated a healthy taking of bookings. With my cards now printed, I hope to talk to a few running clubs, colleges and universities. I spoke at two primary schools recently. The first one was Bygrove Primary in East London where the year-four pupils had been doing projects about mountains. It was great interacting with the children, showing my equipment and getting them to point where mountains were on the globe. There is no hiding from children. They ask what they want. They had even prepared a list of questions. I witnessed only one big yawn at the beginning. I thought it was funny, but it could have been quite off-putting so early on in the presentation, especially as the little girl got up to do it.

The second talk was at my niece's Roman Catholic primary school in Charing. Unfortunately, Mia was both not allowed and not old enough to hear her uncle speak. I got the impression she was quite disappointed. This talk was more formal and I felt I did not have the same interaction with the children. They were sitting in rows as though they were at the cinema (as opposed to tables scattered around the classroom). I could only interact with the children at the front but it did not stop them asking a whole host of questions. The children addressed the teachers as Mr, Mrs and Miss. They called me Mr Buckingham which felt rather plummy, dated and boarding school-ish. The teachers addressed each other by their surnames too. I was not impressed that they kept interrupting me during my presentation. I felt it showed poor manners. It all seemed like such an act, reminding me of a sketch from the comedy *Little Britain*. But I am not put off easily and would happily do the talk again; I was just not prepared for it. I am still hoping young Freya Phelps will work on her teachers and get me into Landulph Primary School. Perhaps I should give her one of my printed cards. I have even opened a local climbing wall in Saltash at the K2 centre – an excellent opportunity to give young people a chance in a safe environment with expert instruction on hand.

Mountain climbing has been an education. I call it 'my fifteen-year degree'. At school, by my own admission, I underachieved, but this gave me the impetus to work hard and methodically tick off each 'module' as I went along, learning new skills and putting them into practice. Even writing this book has been a new challenge, researching, note-taking and flicking through albums of photos looking for inspiration to put into words. I have not written so much since school. In the early days, I tried to write too much in one go and ended up reverting to note form. Over the course of time, I have learnt to limit the number of pages I write before taking a break.

Think what you will of me. If you have never known or met me, I would say that I am a humble person, not big-headed or arrogant in any way. If I have earned some dignity and respect, then it is all well and good. Any challenge I undertake is considered, thought out and executed to the best of my ability. What the future holds nobody knows. In life, there is no written manual and no set of rules. People who criticise are generally those who are too afraid to have a go.

CHAPTER 15

MUD, SWEAT AND THE PENIS GOURD

It was the finest singing I had ever heard,
with all the Dani involved in a sophisticated
symphony of solo and chorus.

— DOUG SCOTT

'I should stay inside the house. We will not be going anywhere soon. Seeing you all could incite the situation further', were the words of Meldy Senduk, a Papua guide from the travel company Adventure Indonesia. I was in a situation not uncommon in Papua New Guinea; heated arguments, blockades, machete and bow-and-arrow-bearing tribesmen are a way of life there. Although the vehemence was not directly targeted at us clients, myself and eighteen others were stuck in the middle of it. The exchanges were directed at our Papua guides and our tour guides from Adventure Indonesia. Their limited resource of money to employ only a handful of porters from the local villages of Sugapa did not sit well with these people, as we found numerous times. Given time, the onset of a torrential downpour and, of course, a payoff, standoffs were diffused.

The local tribal people were called the Dani. Noted for their attire, the menfolk often wore no more than a penis gourd or Kepewak. They did not share many of the accepted norms of modern Western culture. They quite happily strutted around showing off their upright manhood and they posed for photos without expression. The Dani are traditionally a warrior nation but the worst inter-tribal feuds ended with the arrival of missionaries in the 1950s. Now most practise Christianity and have a quiet dignified demeanor. The men and women live in huts called Ebei (women's hut) and Honai (men's hut), which have circular walls made from bark or wood topped by a heavily thatched grass roof. Their possessions are very basic. Until the 1950s they lived in total primitive isolation without wheeled transport. Sweet potato is their staple diet though most people would appreciate it being cooked for longer. The Dani rear pigs, which they take better care of than their dogs. They are adept at catching birds and other animals for food. The western Dani, unlike their neighbours to the east and south of Carstensz, have no recent confirmed history of cannibalism.

Yes, I was on an expedition again, ten months after being in Antarctica. Chris from Vinson had convinced me to make the journey to a politically unstable part of the world. Yes, I had claimed the seven summits but Carstensz Pyramid makes a valid case for being included among the seven summits because it is the highest mountain in Australasia. Carstensz is roughly the same height as Vinson. Neither mountain was the most difficult challenge I faced but both were experiences nonetheless.

If you had lived in Holland in the early seventeenth century you would have joined fellow countrymen in ridiculing Dutch navigator, Jan Carstensz, who claimed that on a voyage across the south-east Pacific, in 1623, he had seen snow-capped mountains only four degrees off the equator. At 4,884 metres, Carstensz Pyramid is the highest mountain in Irian Jaya. If calculations are based on continental platforms, rather than plate tectonics, it is the highest mountain in Australasia. Carstensz lies, according to local tribal language, in the Dugundugu, the high mountains in what was formerly known as Dutch New Guinea, the second largest island in the world. The pyramid is a long, rocky fin, one of several 4,000-metre summits that make up the Sudirman Range. The primitive inhabitants to the south refer to these peaks rather more delightfully as the Namangkawee, or 'Mountains of the White Arrow'. It is the highest island mountain chain in the world.

Carstensz is a remote peak which is difficult to access. Until the quest to collect the seven summits took off in the late 1980s, it received relatively scant attention. It is not the most demanding climb of the seven summits but it is the most technical of them all. Many years ago, the permanent ice cover descended as low as 2,000 metres but, like other mountains, it has seen dramatic glacial recession. Similar to Kilimanjaro, the ice barely drops below 4,200 metres and the highest valleys are desolate with exposed glaciated slabs and moraines.

Virtually all the climbing on Carstensz takes place on the vast North Face of the mountain, a slabby angle averaging no more than seventy-five to eighty degrees, rising about 600 metres above the Yellow Valley. Although there is loose rock in the gullies, on the open faces the rock is immaculate. Aggressively abrasive, it is advisable to wear thin gloves or extensive taping to the hands when climbing. When the Dutch finally withdrew from the island in 1963, they hoped that the country called West Papua would be able to implement a programme of self-rule. However, over the next five years, the administration of the Indonesian Republic 'persuaded' the people to accept a new government. From 1965 to the present day, the Organisasi Papua Merdeka (OPM), the Free Papua Movement, has waged a nearly constant, but so far futile, guerrilla war against Indonesian rule. In 1973, the country was formally renamed Irian Jaya Irianis an acronym from the political slogan, 'The Indonesian Republic in the struggle against the Netherlands'. Jaya means 'victory'. The area was closed to foreigners for most of the nineties due to political unrest but by 1999 the situation had stabilised. The first climbers allowed back into the region made a successful ascent of Carstensz in February 1999.

Apart from the financial commitment, which was small fry compared to Everest and Vinson, the weather was the greatest deterrent to my journey. After negotiating the complex approach, a climber can experience rain at any time, not light rain, but deluges in the rainforest. I experienced these rains first hand, usually at the same time of day, for around two hours. The minimal wind and humidity felt refreshing at times. Wide disbelief in Jan Carstensz's observations continued for almost 300 years. In 1910, an expedition that included Dr A.F. Wollaston, later an Everest explorer, set out from the south coast of New Guinea. Forcing a route through swamps, jungles and dense forest took time and effort. After almost a year, the party gave up after just sixty-four kilometres from the peak. Wollaston returned in the summer of 1912/1913 and overcame considerable hardship to reach the initial ice slopes of the mountain.

In 1936, the Royal Netherlands Geographical Society sponsored Dr A.H. Colyn and two companions in another attempt to climb the island's highest peak. They climbed Ngga Pulu which they thought was the highest of the Sudirman Peaks due to the much thicker glacier ice that then covered the summit. With the rapid shrinking of the region's glaciers, the rocky summit, Carstensz, has since been found to be higher. Later calculations revealed their mistake. War then broke out and throughout the 1950s the Himalaya and Andes were the focal point of mountain exploration. It wasn't until 1960 that climbers began to think seriously of Carstensz once more. The following year, New Zealand alpinist Philip Temple and four fellow enthusiasts found a route to the foot of the North Face, only to return disappointed when their proposed airdrop failed to materialise. Temple had the chance to return six months later with legendary mountaineer, Heinrich Harrer who was a veteran of the first ascent of the Eiger's

North Face. Also recruited was Australian rock-climber Russell Kippax and Dutch patrol officer, Albert Huizenga. This time the airdrop went as planned and the group climbed thirty-three summits, including the first ascent of Carstensz Pyramid. The route is now known as the Normal Route via the North Face and upper West Ridge. On 13 February 1962, they all reached the summit on their first attempt, which was impressive particularly for Huizenga who had never climbed before.

After recovering from frostbite, sustained on Nanga Parbat in 1970, Reinhold Messner made the second ascent. This was via the East Ridge. Twelve months later a Hong Kong-based British team, which included Jack Baines, Dick Isherwood and Leo Murray, were the first to venture on to the excellent limestone of Carstensz's North Face. Since then, eleven routes or variations have been created on the north-facing walls of the peak. In 1978, Pete Boardman and his future wife, Hilary Collins, completed Wollaston's unfinished trip by climbing the rotten rock and ice of the South Face to complete the first south-to-north traverse of the mountain.

Carstensz can be approached from the north or south. Early expeditions approached via the southern route, which was closest to the coast. From 1954, previously unexplored valleys to the north-east were opened up and many grass landing strips cleared. Ilaga is the closest village to Carstensz, at a distance of approximately sixty kilometres as the crow flies. A charter flight from either Nabire or Wamena now avoids the worst of the jungle. Ilaga, a highland village with approximately 15,000 inhabitants, is a six-day walk from Base Camp with porters. This is the route we took. The route passes through rain forest and large areas of equatorial bog to reach the uneven limestone plateau. Even though I was wearing wellingtons, the mud and bog still managed to rise over the top and soak my feet. Finally, the route crosses New Zealand Pass and descends to Base Camp by the lakes in the Upper Meren Valley. Aptly named, this pass reminded me strongly of the Tongariro Crossing that I walked with my brother on holiday in New Zealand. It then takes an hour to reach the start of the Normal Route on the North Face. Having reached the tranquil, remote Meren valley, below Carstensz Pyramid, mountaineers today will be faced with the incongruous sound of throbbing machinery. An accompanying geologist, in the 1936 expedition, was the first to notice the unusually rich copper deposits on Ertsberg, a neighbouring 4,100-metre peak north-west of Carstensz. Mining rights were acquired by a New Orleans-based company. The site is now the largest opencast copper mine in the world and reportedly has the largest gold deposits. Operating the mine required building a deep water port on the south coast, an airstrip and construction of nearly 130 kilometres of access road. When the mine is receptive to visitors (which is seldom) the road provides fast access for climbers, just three hours from Base Camp. There is still scope for more new routes on the North Face and almost infinite potential for good rock-climbing elsewhere in the range. Due to time and the expense needed to obtain the necessary permits, most visitors now use the experienced commercial operators.

Carstensz is the least visited of the seven summits but it is one of the most seriously affected by littering. Second only I think to Kilimanjaro but, in Kilimanjaro's defence, visitor numbers are far greater. Litter lines the trails and camp deforestation is on the increase because the Dani use firewood for cooking in the camps. Toilet facilities are non-existent. A crap-anywhere policy is prevalent. At Base Camp, rubbish is bagged up and tin cans are left in a fire, but whose responsibility is it to take away? Although the mountain lies within a National Park, there is little evidence of a park authority presence. Future climbing parties, therefore, need to take the initiative and protect the mountain's trails and camps. I find it startling that a major copper mine lies within close proximity. Some consider the area an environmental disaster due to massive deforestation and contamination of natural waterways. The Freeport mine is literally removing mountains to reach valuable mineral ore. It is similar to green fields in England being swallowed up in the constant drive to build more houses. It is hoped that such devastation so close to Carstensz will not discourage visitors from having a responsible attitude to the environment, at present that is clearly not happening. On our expedition, I witnessed members dropping litter on the ground.

Szczepan and I were the last two clients waiting for a motorcycle ride from Sugapa to the start of the trek, at Suanggama Village, forty minutes away. We wondered whether we would ever leave the village. Szczepan was one of five Poles in our group. He and two of his compatriots showed strength far above the rest. Eventually, from the gloom and cloud of late afternoon, two sets of headlights appeared. Slipping behind the riders of our respective motorbikes, we were finally on our way, riding pillion. Winding our way out of the village, we rode into the rural and tranquil surrounding hills and rain forests. A nervy start to say the least, I gripped the rear bike frame as it made its way up and down hill. The conditions were becoming increasingly harder as we drove over sodden, muddy ground. The potentially treacherous wet conditions were making riding difficult for the drivers. I tried to make it clear that I wanted the driver to keep his eyes fixed firmly on the road ahead, rather than keep turning around to check I was still clinging on, but the language barrier made our communication more difficult. I was petrified of letting go of the bike frame. I'm sure I had never signed up for this.

About five minutes from the village, we were scrambling up a hill when the bike began to descend into the mud. The weight of both of us was too much to prevent the bike sinking. We could hear the engine dying, much like a climber drawing on his last breath. The inevitable happened as the engine lost its power and ground to a halt. Stuck in the mud, the bike and

I fell to the left. Very much in slow motion, I was plonked in the wet mud, plastering my left side and christening my clean-on shorts and brand new wellingtons on the very first day. In the coming days, we got very used to the mud. There was a heavy downpour each day for around two hours but there was minimal wind and it was very humid. Until we reached Base Camp, we only had the option of bathing in a stream or wiping ourselves as best we could. Stepping gingerly, without the assistance of my poles, I walked the last few yards to the village along the muddy footpath. The porters had set out late from Sugapa so they were some way behind us, carrying clients' luggage. As it was now very dark and raining persistently, only six clients received their luggage that evening. Just two tents were erected outside a villager's hut. The rest of us spent the night in our sodden, soaked clothes on the wooden floor of the hut. We received a meagre offering of food in the form of a hardly cooked sweet potato. I remember seeing a few members huddled round a stove, savouring the heat and trying to dry out clothes. Weary from international travel and an inauspicious start to the trek, I settled down as best I could, wondering what other delights Papua would have to offer.

CHAPTER 16

THE TRUE SEVENTH SUMMIT

Having climbed both claimed summits, in my belief
Carstensz is the true seventh summit of Australasia.

— ED BUCKINGHAM

Rising early the next morning, I gently massaged the soreness and stiffness out of my weary body. It felt as though I had walked for about eight hours the previous day, carrying a heavy pack and trudging through snow. Stretching, I looked out at my surroundings, as if I needed a reminder. This hotel would not get a very good accommodation rating on TripAdvisor. Rubbing my eyes and smiling ruefully, I stepped outside. It was about 5.30 a.m. and under clear skies the sun was rising. During our trek, the sun was at its strongest in the morning until midday and then it clouded over until the rain came. I soon learnt the best time for drying was in the morning while having breakfast and packing up camp. I walked around the back of the hut to the source of noise that had finally disturbed my troubled night. Three puppies were playfully fighting each other, each squeaking above the other like siblings do over territory. They were not very old and although they were cute, I held back from touching or cradling them through fear of catching rabies. As I took in my surroundings, I saw the expanse of rain forest protruding out of the mist and cloud. Steam was rising after the previous night's downpour like steam coming out of a liner's funnel. The lush green vegetation was never deprived of water.

Apart from distant birds chattering, I could hear nothing. As I turned back, I saw the route we had taken through the quagmire the previous evening. It was very muddy and slippery. Two lone, yellow, brand-new Lafuma tents now stood perched on top of the mud. The porters had managed to erect them in the pouring rain and gloom, before succumbing to exhaustion. I smiled, thinking the tents were probably more comfortable than the hut in which I had spent the night. By now, the rest of the team were stumbling out of the hut to take in their surroundings in the cold light of day. The guides had also risen and were preparing breakfast in a tent adjacent to the hut. As it was now sunny, tables were erected outside and a feast was spread out, consisting of rice, cabbage, sausages, fried fish, chips and cheese-breaded balls. The cynical side of me thought they were making a special effort after the fiasco of the night before but, during the following days, this became the norm. We were expected to make a packed lunch to last the day, until we ate again in the evening. The clients zoomed in on the food like vultures. Dr Jan commented to me, 'Watching you lot eat was like watching a load of carnivorous animals eating.' Unfortunately, while we were eating, the villagers had risen and had surrounded our paddock and route to the forest. One of the tribesmen made a rallying speech, which bonded the wall around us even further. We were trapped again, much like the previous day. It felt like the scene in the film *Zulu* where the compound is surrounded by natives. I was only hoping we would not suffer a similar fate to Michael Caine and his soldiers. Only a few of the tribesmen were vociferous in their actions towards us, shouting and waving their machetes. The rest remained muted and quiet, seemingly embarrassed by their actions.

Canadian climber, Sandra, who was hoping to complete the seven summits, was sleeping in a tent in the middle of the melee. Sandra had been fortunate to receive all her luggage the previous evening, forfeiting a night of luxury accommodation on the hard floor of the hut. Poking her head out, she was greeted by angry villagers and Dani men wearing penis gourds. Hastily, she scuttled to the rest of us in fear of being taken hostage. Again, we had to remain in camp until peace talks broke out and the crowd dispersed, allowing us to make our escape. Finally, we were on our way. Leaving the village and arguments behind, we were now faced with different hazards: the forest mud, the vegetation and the fallen tree branches. We had to concentrate on where we placed our feet and make sure our poles did not get caught up in the undergrowth. The poles were a godsend for this trek. It was preferable to use two of them. At times, we had to yank them out from behind us when they became stuck in the thick mud or tree roots. Mine bent a little but I was thankful I did not have carbon fibre poles. Unfortunately for Samuel Short, an engineer from England, one of his brand new poles broke in the first few days. He had to apply black tape regularly and manage for the rest of the trip. Though we were not feeling the full force of the sun, we still felt the humidity. Wearing a light, buttoned, long-sleeved shirt and shorts, I perspired heavily. By the end of the trek, I was noticeably drinking more fluid to replenish what I had lost. I wondered how my feet would cope in wellingtons, thinking back to when I had bad eczema from wearing boots on the farm. Each day I washed, dried and applied talc meticulously before putting on dry socks. It was noticeably quiet in the forest, just the clients and the porters of which there were fifty-three. The porters also brought their wives and offspring, making it a family vacation.

We crossed rivers that were not particularly swollen with heavy rain but there was evidence of huge gullies carved out when they had flooded. There were bridges over some of the rivers but sometimes we had to tight-rope across a crudely laid tree branch. The more elaborate bridges were erected with sides and a canopy, offering protection from the elements. The first camp was called Honai Payung, at 2,600 metres. It was difficult to say whether we had made any height as there was so much up and down during the day's walk. Because of our late departure, we had not made the progress the guides desired. Walking for around four hours, we had only travelled eight kilometres. The camp site was in a cleared area of the rain forest. Usually there would be a wooden frame lashed together with vines but the Dani people were in the habit of simply throwing tarpaulin over the top and constructing the outside and ends with tree branches. Inside, the floor would be covered with a bed of ferns. The occupants were so tightly packed together that it was cosy until a fire was lit, when smoke started billowing around. The absence of a chimney made the atmosphere unbearable. As in Africa, sunset came early in the evening so late nights were not practical. Having withdrawn into my tent for the night, I was treated to the Dani singing in a sophisticated symphony of solo and chorus.

Over the next three days, we covered a variety of terrain and vegetation. Once we had passed through the forests, we crossed heathland and swamps. Although it was a quicker route across the heathland, it was wet, boggy and surprisingly sandy in places. In the squelch-squelch of the mud, it very much felt like we were taking 'two steps forward, one step back'. Even though the days were not long, it was some of the hardest trekking I have done. I cannot emphasise enough that concentration was imperative in the rainforest.

We got our first glimpse of Mount Carstensz and Puncak Jaya, the highest summit on the mountain. Puncak Jaya is what the locals named the rapidly receding snow-capped mountain of glacier and ice before Jan Carstensz made his discovery. Today the receding snow looks like a flat cap slipping off a forehead. What did surprise me was the relative lack of insect life. Though I was prepared for mosquito bites, I received none.

I got more once I was back in Bali. Going through rivers and streams, and at times going up and in over my wellingtons, I expected leeches. With all the lush, and sometimes long, vegetation, I also expected to find ticks. Checking after bathing each evening, I found none. When I say bathing, I mean wet wipes and water from my bottle. During these days, the group split up according to their walking speeds. The three Poles, Slawomir, Babij and Szczepan were the quickest. They route marched and only stopped for a short respite every couple of hours. I learnt that Babij was a builder and Slawomir was a doctor, who ran ultra-marathons. Amusingly, Szczepan wore one wellington and one Gore-Tex walking boot. He explained that one was for speed and the other was for the wet. As I got to know the rest of the group, I realised how experienced everybody was. We were a mix of eleven nationalities and we had twelve Everest summits between us. Everybody, it seemed, was on the seven summit circuit. Robert from Holland and Unai from Spain were on Everest the same year as me. In fact, when I spoke to Unai about our respective expeditions on Everest, we realised we had passed within thirty minutes of each other. But how can you expect to recognise someone behind an oxygen mask, cocooned in a down hood at almost 8,850 metres? The two older members were Huig from Holland (seventy) and Dr Jan (seventy-two) from Australia. As a retirement hobby, Huig had decided to try for the seven summits, even though he had no real mountaineering experience. He had a long way to go with Everest, Denali and Aconcagua, which were certainly the most difficult, still to conquer. However, there were signs that made me believe he would never get there. On this trip so far, he had already fallen into the river and he was always the last into camp, accompanied by at least three guides. Dr Jan took three attempts to climb Everest. Successful on her third attempt, she became one of the oldest women to summit (at the age of seventy). Although she had two failed attempts on Aconcagua and Denali, she had every intention of going back within the next twelve months. My money was on Dr Jan to succeed first.

We arrived at Nasidome, Riverside Camp. The next day saw a dramatic scenery change as we went over the New Zealand Pass to Base Camp. From Nasidome, we walked up a rocky path to the top where we looked down on to Larson Lake which nestled in among the mountains. It was so tranquil and peaceful, there was not even a ripple across the surface. Scanning around, we could see the landscape had become more mountainous. For the next few hours, we climbed up mountain passes. I could now feel the stones through my rapidly wearing wellingtons. Have I mentioned the importance of buying dearer equipment and not cutting corners? Even though it was raining, the white path remained hard, winding its way up to the New Zealand Pass, at 4,500 metres. The New Zealand Pass was the highest point we reached that day, before descending into Base Camp. Upon reaching the pass, I looked directly at Carstensz and the rocky limestone walls we would climb. Looking down, I saw other smaller lakes which were emerald turquoise in colour. They shone bright in the sunshine but not today in the dull and dreary weather. Looking at one end of the valley, I could see into the Freeport mine.

Descending down the steep rocky paths, we had to be careful not to slip, twist a knee or an ankle. Base Camp was beside an emerald lake, rich in minerals and ore. Carstensz flanked the lake. There was no mistaking where we were. An old iron sign creaked on a post reading, 'Base Camp 4,300m'. As I surveyed the camp site, I observed that it was situated on hard ground and I could see the remains of campfires. Tin cans and rubbish tied up in plastic bags caught my eye and put a blot on the landscape. I think it's completely unnecessary and could easily be rectified by park authority enforcement. We spent three nights at Base Camp. This was our chance to rest and to dry out. The walk to Base Camp had been the worst so far, with persistent rain every day. We were split into two summit groups consisting of nine and ten clients. We travelled on separate days, providing us with a rest day, the only one of the trip. It is unusual to walk on consecutive days. It meant a change of footwear to walking boots, the only day I wore them.

I was in the first group, leaving on the morning of the nineteenth of November. The early-morning start was tropical compared to some of the other mountains. It was cloudy and warm at around ten degrees. I only wore two layers of thermal clothing and a Gore-Tex shell. Apart from when we were climbing on the abrasive rock, we did not need gloves. It took us one hour to get to the foot of Carstensz. Worryingly, it started raining but thankfully it stopped within half an hour. The previous day had seen the worst weather so far, raining steadily for most of the day. With no time to dry ourselves, many of us still had damp clothing on. Leaving the poles at the bottom, we started climbing by fixing ourselves on to the ropes and using a Jumar, a device used when ascending a rope. The teeth grip into the rope, allowing a climber to put their full weight on it. To progress higher, a climber simply slides the Jumar up the rope and repeats the process. It was tricky for us to negotiate a big lump of rock to start with, having to stretch ourselves round to the side. It reminded me of the first step on Everest but, of course, at a significantly lower altitude. Dawn was breaking now so we did not need our head torches. We had only been wearing them for a couple of hours. The rock was good to climb, offering plenty of good foot and handholds, which I gripped on to with confidence. The rock did not crumble and I was able to propel myself upwards. Resting on a ledge, I could see into the Freeport mine again. The excavation into the mountainside was massive. Carrying on up, I climbed a gullied section, like a chimney, which offered protection from the wind, if there had been any.

In preparation for this day, I had spent time climbing at Symonds Yat in the Wye Valley, England with Alec Roberts of Guided Mountain. As the day wore on, some of the routes became harder and I did not complete them. My body became tired because I was exercising muscles I didn't usually use. Consequently, I made decisions I would not have, had I not been so tired. What I did achieve on that invaluable day's experience stood me in good stead for Carstensz. It would not surprise me if one day I return to Symonds Yat to attempt the failed routes again, but next time, I would wear rock shoes. A motto I use is, 'If at first you don't succeed then try again'.

Reaching the top of this long gully, we came out on to the ridge leading to the summit. We were all doing well. The three Poles charged ahead on the fixed ropes. With the summits and altitudes we had experienced, this would not be a problem for any of us. Standing up on the ridgeline, we could now see both sides of the mountain, either side of the cloud. We could look across at the pass we came over yesterday. We could make out a yellow helicopter dropping supplies at Base Camp, replenishing the two tonnes of food we had started out with.

Handrailing across the ridge, we came to the biggest obstacle on the summit push, 'The Tyrolean Traverse'. Two steel cables went across a gorge from one point to the other. Once one guide went across, a third rope was used as a pulley to help the clients. Standing in a queue awaiting my turn, I felt slightly nervous, like I did when I crossed the crevasses on Everest. I knew if I did not quell my nerves, my efforts would be in vain. Once it came to my turn, it did not feel so bad as I slid my hands and feet across with my back facing downwards. Though I am not noted for my hand and foot co-ordination, I was surprisingly quite good at this. With the help of the guides using the third rope as a pulley, soon everyone was safely across with both feet on firm ground. It was then a relatively safe passage to the summit. We handrailed either side of the mountain, along a path before a steep scramble to the summit. Babij, Slawomir, Samuel, Szczepan and Unai had just got there ahead of me.

At around 8 a.m. I claimed my eighth summit in my seven summits conquest. No disputing any claims now. I had visited Australasia twice. We were soon joined by Atanas, Ricardo, Monika and the guides. Poxi (the most experienced climber and leader of this expedition), Josh and Meds had accompanied us and now we all crowded at the small summit. There was no mistaking the summit, as there was a small plaque with scripture written on it. Alongside it was a memorial photo of a climber who had perished on the mountain – a reminder of what can happen. This was Poxi's fiftieth summit, with a 100 per cent success rate. He had made all his summits in his wellington boots, never bothering to carry walking boots. He attained the nickname 'The Cat' because of the way he bounced from foot to foot, cowering slightly and prowling like a feline. Once we were all on top, clients had their photographs taken with banners. Josh pulled out some banners printed by Adventure Expeditions. Among the banners there was a group one for the Poles and group banner for the guides, one celebrating Poxi's fiftieth summit and a special individual one for me. Mine was to congratulate the fact I had completed the 'Real Seven Summits'. I was touched that the company had made the effort to produce a personalised memento. It is a memory I shall treasure from this long adventure. I am not sure I have a wall long enough to hang the banner. Samuel and I had to hold one end each so a photo could be taken. Sandra and Youngjo received their personalised banners the next day. For his summit photo, Poxi took things a step further by stripping off and posing in his purple leotard and yellow pants, grinning from ear to ear. I decided against doing this, fearing my underwear was not as clean. There was no rush to go down as it was very sunny now with no wind.

We must have been up there approaching two hours which was by far the longest I had spent on any summit.

Eventually we did descend back the same way we came, into the very warm valley of Base Camp. It was the warmest day so far and the journey had taken us nine and a half hours. It was quite a comfortable quick summit considering the time spent on top and the time we had spent waiting to cross the traverse. The next day, the second group of clients made a successful summit attempt while we rested. The slightly windier conditions slowed them down but they all made the summit. Huig was the last to return, accompanied by four guides. Dismissive of any suggestion that he should reconsider attempting Everest, Denali and Aconcagua, Huig was still going to press ahead with his potentially ill-fated plans. It begs the question, if it took four guides to help him climb Carstensz, how many would he need for Everest? What would this trip cost him? A climber's life? People invest money into trying to ascertain personal glories when quite inconceivably they have very little chance of success. More worryingly, Huig had picked up an infection on his lower leg and hadn't informed anybody. He had scraped it early on in the expedition and it had since become infected, swollen and gangrene-like. With four days trekking back through the rain forest, the outlook was unpromising for him. With no way of keeping the wound clean and dry, there was a real danger of him losing part of his leg unless he sought medical care. On consulting with Slawonir, he took the option of going the quicker route via the Freeport mine and using their hospital. The mine was reluctant to let him pass through at first because many people try to avoid walking through the arduous rain forest. By the time we caught up with him a week later, at the final dinner and awards, he looked like a different man. Strong antibiotics had killed the infection so his leg had gone down in size. He explained that he had received good medical care from American doctors at the hospital. He also said that when he was shipped out to Timika, he went in an armour-plated vehicle so the locals would not see him. He was still adamant he was going to scale the remaining summits.

Dr Jan found the going tougher back through the forest; taking extra care had cost her valuable time. She put in a twelve, followed by a fifteen-hour day. She was plucky and fiercely determined, even when she lost her glasses in a swollen river. On the way back, she also received scrapes and cuts to her lower leg, which became infected. Back in Bali, they were tended to immediately, especially as her trip to Aconcagua was imminent, in early January 2015. In truth, several of us suffered where our boots rubbed and our lower legs got wet.

Back on the motorcycles from Suanggama Village in the pouring rain, there was time for one last blockade. This was something I had not missed. Although the villagers let us through, they followed us back to Sugapa. Knowing that we were flying out the next day, they demanded money before they let us through. Some would say this was greedy, as we had already paid good money for their handcrafted wares, like the penis gourd, the afternoon before. What topic of conversation or party games could involve the penis gourd back home?

A few days later, while I was relaxing, drinking cocktails in Bali, I allowed myself a moment of reflection. Chris was right, it had been an experience like no other, in a developing country where the trekking, people and culture were so different. The altitude, at just under 5,000 metres, was never going to truly affect me, as by then I was fitter than when I climbed Cho Oyu and Everest. The climb itself was different from anything else I had experienced, offering a proper rock-climb rather than a walk to the summit. Ten years after I had summited Kilimanjaro, I returned again. Could I see myself one day return to Papua New Guinea, smiling and chuckling? No.

ACKNOWLEDGEMENTS

Top of the list are obviously my parents for bringing me into this world and raising me as the man I am today, and for the love, care, patience and guidance they gave me. A special mention must be given to time as well: my parents always gave me the time of day, a precious commodity. I think it can often be overlooked in today's hectic modern society. I know on the odd occasion I may have given you a few worrying hours, but I do remember the words, 'we would never step in the way of you wanting to do something'.

Next I must also mention my brother and his family. As kids, Chris and I used to fight like tigers but thankfully, as he put it, 'Ed grew up'. Mia, Jessica and Theo are a joy to be with and I often think of them when I am away. Rebecca, my sister-in-law, deserves a special mention for her input into my book and for never quite getting round to writing my synopsis.

My Uncle Ray through being out in the community has got me several presentations and nominated me to open Quiethock Show in July 2014.

Fiona Phelps I met in Tamar Trotters. When she heard that I was writing a book her support was amazing. Despite having a family of her own and a demanding job Fiona still managed to find the time to type the chapters up for me. Her quirky little Post-it notes made me laugh each time my work came back. Fiona never hesitated in bugging me for more work to type up. I appreciate her competitiveness in running and her enthusiasm while I was writing this book.

The rest of the acknowledgements are made up of people, associations and businesses that have helped me in writing this book, in no particular order. Patrick Loxdale, Bev Derrick, Arnold Coster, Andy Sloan, Tenji Sherpa, Jemima Lang, Rob and Jo Gambi, Niki Stewart, Dominic Pickett,

Mark Bellamy, Alec Roberts, Matt George, Dr Webster Harrison and Barbara Shaw.

The businesses and associations that have helped me are: Royal Mail, Trematon WI, British Heart Foundation, Cotswold Outdoor, Western Morning News, Cornish Times, Landrake Young Farmers, Tamar Trotters, Kathmandu Medical Centre, Vertebrate Publishing, Caradon and Restormel Ramblers, Adventure Peaks and Summit Climb.

I apologise if I have missed anyone. I have met some wonderful people during this venture, from all walks of life and backgrounds, especially in mess tents talking over cocoa. I have also had a lot of fun and support talking to children in primary schools and, as in life, you never know what to expect next from them.

I hope you enjoyed this book.